GREAT WRITING

FIFTH EDITION
Keith S. Folse
April Muchmore-Vokoun
Elena Vestri

NATIONAL GEOGRAPHIC
LEARNING

Australia · Brazil · Mexico · Singapore · United Kingdom · United States

Great Writing 2: Great Paragraphs
Keith S. Folse, April Muchmore-Vokoun, Elena Vestri

Publisher: Sherrise Roehr

Executive Editor: Laura Le Dréan

Senior Development Editor: Eve Einselen Yu

Director of Global Marketing: Ian Martin

Product Marketing Manager: Tracy Bailie

Senior Director, Production: Michael Burggren

Production Manager: Daisy Sosa

Content Project Manager: Mark Rzeszutek

Manufacturing Planner: Mary Beth Hennebury

Art Director: Brenda Carmichael

Interior Design: Lisa Trager

Cover Design: Lisa Trager

Composition: SPi-Global

Student Edition: 978-0-357-02083-8
Student Edition with Online Workbook Access Code: 978-0-357-02106-4

National Geographic Learning
20 Channel Center Street
Boston, MA 02210
USA

Cengage learning is a leading provider of customized learning solutions with office locations around the globe, including Singapore, the United Kingdom, Australia, Mexico, Brazil, and Japan. Locate our local office at: **International. cengage.com/region**

Cengage Learning products are represented in Canada by Nelson Education, Ltd.

Visit NGL online at **ELTNGL.com**

Visit our corporate website at **cengage.com**

Printed in China
Print Number: 01   Print Year: 2018

CONTENTS

GREAT WRITING MAKES GREAT WRITERS

The new edition of *Great Writing* provides clear explanations, academic writing models, and focused practice to help students write great sentences, paragraphs, and essays. Every unit has expanded vocabulary building, sentence development, and more structured final writing tasks.

National Geographic images and content spark students' imaginations and inspire their writing.

Each unit includes:

PART 1: **Elements of Great Writing** teaches the fundamentals of writing.

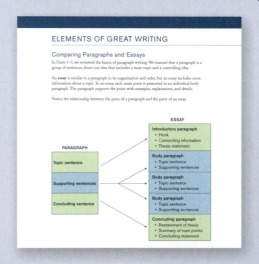

Writing Models encourage students to analyze and use the features of great writing in their own work.

Targeted Grammar presents clear explanations and examples that students can immediately apply to their work.

PART 2: Building Better Vocabulary highlights academic words, word associations, collocations, word forms, and vocabulary for writing.

New Words to Know boxes throughout each unit target carefully-leveled words students will frequently use.

PART 3: Building Better Sentences focuses students on sentence-level work to ensure more accurate writing.

PART 4: Writing activities allow students to apply what they have learned by guiding them through the process of writing, editing, and revising.

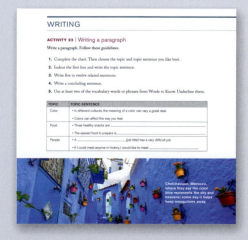

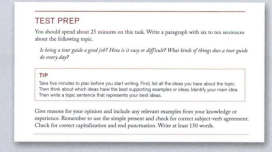

NEW Test Prep section prepares students for timed writing on high-stakes tests.

SUPPORT FOR INSTRUCTORS AND STUDENTS

FOR INSTRUCTORS

The Classroom Presentation Tool brings the classroom to life by including all Student Book pages, answers, and games to practice vocabulary.

Assessment: ExamView allows instructors to create custom tests and quizzes in minutes. **ExamView** and **Ready to Go Tests** are available online at the teacher companion website for ease of use.

FOR STUDENTS

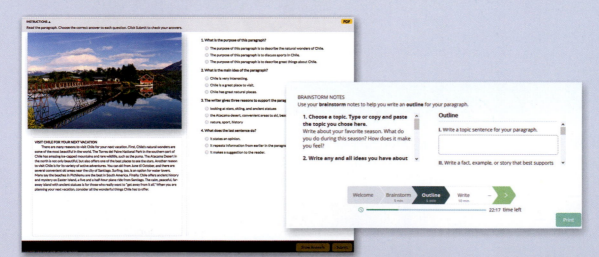

The Online Workbook provides additional practice in vocabulary, grammar, and writing, plus remediation activities for students who have not mastered at-level vocabulary and grammar.

NEW Guided online writing practice reinforces the writing process, helping students become stronger and more independent writers.

ACKNOWLEDGEMENTS

The Authors and Publisher would like to acknowledge and thank the teachers around the world who participated in the development of the fifth edition of *Great Writing*.

Asia

Anthony Brian Gallagher, Meijo University, Nagoya

Atsuko Aoki, Aoyama Gakuin University, Tokyo

Atsushi Taguchi, Okayama University of Science, Imabari Campus, Ehime

Helen Hanae, Reitaku University, Kashiwa

Hiroko Shikano, Juchi Medical University, Gotemba

Hisashi Shigematsu, Toyo Gakeun University, Tokyo

Jeremiah L. Hall, Meijo University, Nagoya

Jian Liang Fu, Kwansei Gakuin University, Nishinomiya

Jim Hwang, Yonsei University, Asan

John C. Pulaski, Chuo University and Tokyo Woman's Christian University, Tokyo

Junyawan Suwannarat, Chiang Mai University, Chiang Mai

Katherine Bauer, Clark Memorial International High School, Chiba

Kazuyo Ishibashi, Aoyama Gakuin Univeristy, Tokyo

Lei Na, Jump A-Z, Nanjing

Lor Kiat Seng, Southern University College, Seremban

Mark McClure, Kansai Gaidai Univeristy, Osaka

Matthew Shapiro, Konan Boys High School, Ashiya

Nattalak Thirachotikun, Chiang Mai University, Chiang Rai

Nick Boyes, Meijo University, Nagoya

Nick Collier, Ritsumeikan Uji Junior and Senior High School, Kobe

Olesya Shatunova, Kanagawa University, Yokohama

Pattanapichet Fasawang, Bangkok University International College, Bangkok

Paul Hansen, Hokkaido University, Sapporo

Paul Salisbury, Aichi University, Nagoya

Randall Cotten, Gifu City Women's College, Gifu

Sayaka Karlin, Toyo Gakuen University, Tokyo

Scott Gray, Clark Memorial International High School Umeda Campus, Osaka

Selina Richards, HELP University, Kuala Lumpur

Terrelle Bernard Griffin, No. 2 High School of East China Normal University-International Division, Shanghai

William Pellowe, Kinki University, Fukuoka

Yoko Hirase, Hiroshima Kokusai Gakuin University, Hiroshima

Youngmi Lim, Shinshu University, Matsumoto

Zachary Fish, RDFZ Xishan School AP Center, Beijing

USA

Amanda Kmetz, BIR Training Center, Chicago, Illinois

Amy Friedman, The American Language Institute, San Diego, California

Amy Litman, College of Southern Nevada, Las Vegas, Nevada

Angela Lehman, Virginia Commonwealth University, Richmond, Virginia

Aylin Bunk, Mount Hood Community College, Portland, Oregon

Barbara Silas, South Seattle College, Seattle, Washington

Bette Brickman, College of Southern Nevada, Las Vegas, Nevada

Breana Bayraktar, Northern Virginia Community College, Fairfax, Virginia

Carolyn Ho, Lone Star College-CyFair, Cypress, Texas

Celeste Flowers, University of Central Arkansas, Conway, Arkansas

Christina Abella, The College of Chicago, Chicago, Illinois

Christine Lines, College of Southern Nevada, Las Vegas, Nevada

Clare Roh, Howard Community College, Columbia, Maryland

DeLynn MacQueen, Columbus State Community College, Columbus, Ohio

Eleanor Molina, Northern Essex Community College, Lawrence, Massachusetts

Emily Brown, Hillsborough Community College, Florida

Emily Cakounes, North Shore Community College, Medford, Massachusetts

Erica Lederman, BIR Training Center, Chicago, Illinois

Erin Zoranski, Delaware Technical Community College, Wilmington, Delaware

Eugene Polissky, University of Potomac, Washington, DC

Farideh Hezaveh, Northern Virginia Community College, Sterling, Virginia

Gretchen Hack, Community College of Denver, Denver, Colorado

Heather Snavely, California Baptist University, Riverside, California

Hilda Tamen, University of Texas Rio Grande Valley, Edinburg, Texas

Holly Milkowart, Johnson County Community College, Overland Park, Kansas

Jessica Weimer, Cascadia College, Bothell, Washington

Jill Pagels, Lonestar Community College, Houston, Texas

Jonathan Murphy, Virginia Commonwealth University, Richmond, Virginia

Joseph Starr, Houston Community College, Southwest, Houston, Texas

Judy Chmielecki, Northern Essex Community College, Lawrence, Massachusetts

Kate Baldridge-Hale, Valencia College, Orlando, Florida

Kathleen Biache, Miami Dade College, Miami, Florida

Katie Edwards, Howard Community College, Columbia, Maryland

Kenneth Umland, College of Southern Nevada, Las Vegas, Nevada

Kevin Bowles, Linfield College, McMinnville, Oregon

Kim Hardiman, University of Central Florida, Orlando, Florida

Kori Zunic, San Diego City College, San Diego, California

Kris Lowrey, Virginia Commonwealth University, Richmond, Virginia

Kristin Homuth, Language Center International, Oak Park, Michigan

Leon Palombo, Miami Dade College, North Campus, Miami Beach, Florida

Lily Jaffie-Shupe, Virginia Polytechnic Institute, Blacksburg, Virginia

Lisse Hildebrandt, Virginia Commonwealth University, Richmond, Virginia

Luba Nesterova, Bilingual Education Institute, Houston, Texas

Madhulika Tandon, Lone Star College, University Park, Houston, Texas

Matthew Wolpert, Virginia Commonwealth University, Richmond, Virginia

Megan Nestor, Seattle Central College, Seattle, Washington

Meredith Kemper, University of Central Arkansas, Conway, Arkansas

Mike Sfiropoulos, Palm Beach State College, Lake Worth, Florida

Milena Eneva, Chattahoochee Technical College, Atlanta, Georgia

Myra M. Medina, Miami Dade College, Miami, Florida

Naomi Klimowicz, Howard Community College, Columbia, Maryland

Nicholas C. Zefran, Northern Virginia Community College, Springfield, Virginia

Nicole Ianieri, East Carolina University, Greenville, North Carolina

Patricia Nation, Miami Dade College, Miami, Florida

Paul Kern, Green River College, Auburn, Washington

Rachel DeSanto, Hillsborough Community College, Tampa, Florida

Ramon Perez, Northern Virginia Community College, Dumfries, Virginia

Rebecca McNerney, Virginia Commonwealth University, Richmond, Virginia

Richard Roy, Middlesex County College, Edison, New Jersey

Sandra Navarro, Glendale Community College, Glendale, California

Shane Dick, College of Southern Nevada, Las Vegas, Nevada

Sheila Mayne, University of Pennsylvania, Philadelphia, Pennsylvania

Stephen Johnson, Miami Dade College, Florida

Sumeeta Patnaik, Marshall University, Huntington, West Virginia

Summer Webb, International English Center, Colorado

Tom Sugawara, University of Washington, Seattle, Washington

Viviana Simon, Howard Community College, Columbia, Maryland

William Albertson, Drexel University, Philadelphia, Pennsylvania

Yu Bai, Howard Community College, Laurel, Maryland

Middle East

Deborah Abbott, Prince Muhammad Bin Fahd University, Al Khobar, Saudi Arabia

Genie Elatili, Prince Muhammad Bin Fahd University, Al Khobar, Saudi Arabia

Julie Riddlebarger, Khalifa University, United Arab Emirates

Karla Moore, Virginia International Private School, Abu Dhabi, United Arab Emirates

Laila AlQadhi, Kuwait University, Kuwait

FROM THE AUTHORS

Great Writing began in 1998 when three of us were teaching writing and frequently found ourselves complaining about the lack of materials for English language learners. A lot of books talked about writing but did not ask the students to write until the end of a chapter. In essence, the material seemed to be more of a lecture followed by "Now you write an essay." Students were reading a lot but writing little. What was missing was useful sequenced instruction for developing ESL writers by getting them to write.

Each of us had folders with our own original tried-and-true activities, so we set out to combine our materials into a coherent book that would help teachers and students alike. The result was *Great Paragraphs* and *Great Essays*, the original books of the *Great Writing* series. Much to our surprise, the books were very successful. Teachers around the world reached out to us and offered encouragement and ideas. Through the past four editions we have listened to those ideas, improved upon the books, and added four more levels.

We are proud to present this 5th edition of the *Great Writing* series with the same tried-and-true focus on writing and grammar, but with an added emphasis on developing accurate sentences and expanding level-appropriate academic vocabulary.

We thank those who have been involved in the development of this series over the years. In particular for the 5th edition, we would like to thank Laura Le Dréan, Executive Editor; the developmental editors for this edition: Lisl Bove, Eve Einselen Yu, Yeny Kim, Jennifer Monaghan, and Tom Jefferies. We will be forever grateful to two people who shaped our original books: Susan Maguire and Kathy Sands-Boehmer. Without all of these professionals, our books would most definitely not be the great works they are right now.

As always, we look forward to hearing your feedback and ideas as you use these materials with your students.

Sincerely,

Keith Folse
April Muchmore-Vokoun
Elena Vestri
David Clabeaux
Tison Pugh

1 | Paragraphs

OBJECTIVES
- Analyze the four main features of a paragraph
- Use the simple present for general facts
- Use correct subject-verb agreement
- Use capitalization and end punctuation correctly
- Write a paragraph

Copacabana beach and cityscape seen from Sugarloaf Mountain at dusk, Rio de Janeiro, Brazil

FREEWRITE | Look at the photo. What can you say about the geography around Rio de Janeiro and the types of activities people might enjoy? Write five to ten sentences.

ELEMENTS OF GREAT WRITING

What Is a Paragraph?

A **paragraph** is a group of sentences. It has a main idea and sentences that support the idea. Paragraphs help writers organize their ideas when writing longer texts, such as essays and research papers. Learning to write a paragraph is an important academic skill.

ACTIVITY 1 | Analyzing a paragraph

Look at the map and read the information. Discuss the questions with your class. Then read the paragraph and answer the questions that follow.

1. Where are Brazil and Chile?
2. Which country has more people? Which is bigger?
3. What is the official language in Brazil? in Chile?

WORDS TO KNOW Paragraph 1.1

contrast: (n) something different or opposite
differ: (v) to be different
majority: (n) more than half
obvious: (adj) clear; easy to understand

population: (n) all of the people living in a specific area
take up: (phr v) to occupy space

Chile
Capital City:
Santiago
Population:
17,216,945
Official Language:
Spanish
Area: 291,932 square miles (756,102 square kilometers)

Brazil
Capital City:
Brasilia
Population:
183,888,841
Official Language:
Portuguese
Area: 3,286,470 square miles (8,511,965 square kilometers)

Lake Pehoe in Torres del Paine National Park, Chile

Brazil and Chile

Brazil and Chile are near each other, but these two South American countries **differ** in geography, **population**, and language. The most **obvious** difference is in geography. As the map shows, Brazil is much larger than Chile. In fact, Brazil **takes up** almost half of South America. In **contrast**, Chile is a long, thin country along the Pacific Ocean. It is only 160 miles (258 kilometers) wide. These two countries also have very different populations. Brazil is home to almost 200 million people, while only about 17 million people live in Chile. Finally, these two countries have different national languages. Like most countries in South America, the **majority** of people in Chile speak Spanish. However, in Brazil most people speak Portuguese. These countries are near each other, but they are clearly different in several important ways.

1. Which three details does this paragraph discuss? Begin with *This paragraph discusses . . .*

_____

_____

2. In your own words, what is the most important difference between Brazil and Chile? Begin with *The most important difference between Brazil and Chile is . . .*

_____

_____

WRITER'S NOTE Words Signaling Contrast

When showing that a new idea is in contrast, or different, from the ones before, use various kinds of contrast connectors (*but, while, in contrast, however, on the other hand*).

These countries may be near each other, **but** they are clearly different in several ways.

Brazil has almost 200 million people, **while** only 17 million live in Chile.

Grammar: Simple Present for General Facts

EXPLANATION	EXAMPLES		
Use the **simple present** to explain something that is a general fact.	People in Chile **speak** Spanish. These two countries **differ** in population.		
Use the base form of the verb for *I, you, we,* and *they* Note: For the verb *be*, use *I* **am**, *You/We/They* **are.**	I You We They Brazilians	**speak**	Portuguese.
Use the *-s* form for *he, she,* and *it* and third-person nouns. Note: For the verb *be*, use *He/She/It* **is.**	He She It A Brazilian	**speaks**	
When a verb ends in a consonant + *y*, change the *-y* to *-i* and add *-es.*	I try → he tr**ies**		
When a verb ends in *-ch, -sh, -ss, -x,* or *-zz,* add *-es.*	pilots watch → a pilot watch**es** janitors wash → a janitor wash**es** people miss → a foreign student miss**es**		

ACTIVITY 2 | Noticing grammar in writing

Look back at Paragraph 1.1 and answer the questions.

1. What are the seven different verbs used in Paragraph 1.1?

   be (is/are), _____

2. Why are these verbs in the simple present?

   _____

ACTIVITY 3 | Writing sentences

Think of a country that you know well. Write five sentences comparing it with the United States or another country. Use Paragraph 1.1 as a guide. Use the simple present.

1. _____

2. _____

3. _____

4. _____

5. _____

ACTIVITY 4 | Analyzing a paragraph

Discuss the questions. Then read the paragraph and answer the questions that follow.

1. What are three things that you can cook by yourself?
2. What are the first two steps that someone has to follow to cook one of the foods you listed in question 1?

WORDS TO KNOW Paragraph 1.2

at least: (phr) the minimum number or amount required

boil: (v) to cook in water at 212°F (100°C)

ingredient: (n) a food item in a recipe

remove: (v) to take away

PARAGRAPH 1.2

An Easy Sandwich

An egg salad sandwich is one of the easiest and most delicious foods to make for lunch. First, **boil** two eggs for five minutes. Take them out of the water. When they are cool, **remove** the shells. Put the eggs in a bowl and use a fork to break them into very small pieces. Next, add three tablespoons of mayonnaise and a little salt and pepper. Mix these **ingredients** well. Put the egg mixture in the refrigerator for **at least** 30 minutes. Finally, put the egg salad between two slices of bread. By following all of these steps, anyone can make this delicious sandwich.

---

1. What is the purpose of this paragraph? Begin with *The purpose of this paragraph is to. . .*

   _____

   _____

2. This paragraph tells readers how to do something step by step. Which word did the writer

   use to introduce the first step? _____ the final step? _____

3. What phrase does the writer use to introduce the conclusion of the paragraph?

   _____

WRITER'S NOTE Sequence Words

When writing instructions or steps in a process, use sequence words, such as: *First, Second, Next, Finally.* Often a comma comes after the sequence word.

   First, boil two eggs for five minutes. **Next**, add three tablespoons of mayonnaise and a little salt and pepper. **Finally**, put the egg salad between two slices of bread.

ACTIVITY 5 | Writing sentences

Write the main steps of a recipe you know. If you need help, look at the sentences in Paragraph 1.2. When you are finished, share your recipe with a partner.

1. _____

2. _____

3. _____

4. _____

5. _____

Four Features of a Good Paragraph

1. **The first line of a paragraph is indented.** Indenting means moving the first line to the right about a half of an inch (1.25 centimeter). On a keyboard, this is about six spaces.
2. **A paragraph has a topic sentence that states the main idea.** The topic sentence is usually at the beginning of a paragraph. It helps the reader understand what the paragraph is about.
3. **All of the sentences in a paragraph are about one topic.** All of the sentences are related to the topic sentence. There are no unrelated or extra sentences.
4. **A paragraph ends with a concluding sentence that brings the paragraph to a logical end.** The concluding sentence usually states the main point again or summarizes the main idea. In addition, it can offer a suggestion, an opinion, or a prediction. It never includes new information. Often a key word or phrase from the topic sentence appears in the concluding sentence.

ACTIVITY 6 | Writing a paragraph

On a separate piece of paper, rewrite your recipe from Activity 5 in the form of a paragraph. Use Paragraph 1.2 as a guide.

ACTIVITY 7 | Analyzing the features of a paragraph

Discuss the questions. Then read the paragraph and answer the questions that follow.

1. Did you have a pet as a child? If yes, what kind of pet did you have? If no, did you want one? Explain.
2. Do you have a pet now? Explain why or why not.

> **WORDS TO KNOW** Paragraph 1.3
>
> **allow:** (v) to permit, let
> **divided:** (adj) having different thoughts/opinions about something
>
> **require:** (v) to need, must have
> **take care of:** (phr v) to watch over

Are Pets a Good Idea?

At some point, parents must decide whether or not to **allow** their children to have pets. Some parents believe that pets teach their children to be responsible because children have to **take care of** their pets. In addition, many parents believe that pets can be fun for the family. On the other hand, some parents are afraid that their children might hurt the animals or that the animals might hurt the children. Cats are good pets, but I do not like it when their hair is on the furniture. Often these parents do not allow their children to have any kind of pet. Other families do not have the time or money that pets **require**. In sum[1], although many children want a pet, parents are **divided** on this topic.

[1]in sum: a phrase used to introduce a summary

1. Is this paragraph indented?   ❏ Yes   ❏ No

2. Underline the topic sentence. What is the main idea of the paragraph? Begin with *The writer wants to explain that...*

_____

_____

3. Find the sentence that is not related to the topic sentence. Cross it out.

4. How many sentences are there in the corrected paragraph? _____

5. Underline the concluding sentence. How is the information in the concluding sentence related to the information in the topic sentence? Begin with *The topic sentence and the concluding sentence both...*

_____

_____

> **WRITER'S NOTE** Topic Sentences
>
> Remember that the topic sentence presents the main idea for the entire paragraph. Always keep this main idea in mind when writing a paragraph.

ACTIVITY 8 | Analyzing the features of Paragraphs 1.1 and 1.2

Look back at Paragraphs 1.1 and 1.2. Answer the questions.

1. Write the topic sentence of each paragraph. Which topic sentence gives a clearer idea of the contents of the paragraph? Tell a partner your ideas.

    "Brazil and Chile": _____

    _____

    "An Easy Sandwich": _____

    _____

2. Write the concluding sentence of each paragraph. Then tell a partner how each one relates to its topic sentence.

    "Brazil and Chile": _____

    _____

    "An Easy Sandwich": _____

    _____

ACTIVITY 9 | Analyzing the features of paragraphs with errors

Read each paragraph and complete the tasks that follow.

> **WORDS TO KNOW** Paragraphs 1.4 to 1.6
>
> **approximately:** (adv) about; more or less
> **attraction:** (n) a place to visit, especially for tourists
> **convenient:** (adj) easy to use
> **convince:** (v) to cause someone to believe something is true
>
> **powerful:** (adj) very strong
> **take place:** (v phr) to happen
> **traditional:** (adj) normal or usual; not new

PARAGRAPH 1.4

e-Readers

For many students, e-readers are better than paper books. First, e-books are better for students' bodies. Before e-readers, students had to carry several heavy books with them each day. However, e-readers are very light and usually weigh less than a pound, so there is less stress on students' bodies. Second, e-readers are more **convenient** than regular books. Students can take all their textbooks with them anywhere they want. They are easy to hold and are clear even in bright sunlight. In addition, reading an e-reader is just like reading a paper book, but they are more convenient because it is not necessary to turn the pages. My friend has an e-reader, and she **convinced** me to buy one. Finally, buying a new e-book often costs less than buying a **traditional** paper book, so students may spend less if they buy e-books. For these reasons, e-readers are better for students than traditional books.

1. Underline the topic sentence in Paragraph 1.4.
2. Find the sentence not related to the topic. Cross it out.
3. Underline the concluding sentence. Then tell a partner how it relates to the topic sentence.

New York City

First, many movies **take place** in New York City, so everyone knows the city even if they have never been there in person. Second, New York City has many famous tourist **attractions**, including the Statue of Liberty, the Empire State Building, Central Park, and Times Square. In addition, the city has some of the best shopping in the world. Finally, New York City is famous for its many theaters with world-class shows. For these reasons, everyone knows about this city.

1. What is the main idea of this paragraph?

   _____

2. Does the paragraph have a topic sentence? If so, write it here. If not, write one here.

   _____

   _____

3. Are all the sentences related to the topic? _____ If not, cross out the unrelated sentence(s).

4. What is the concluding sentence? Underline it.

The Statue of Liberty and New York City under a full moon

11

Statue of Simon Bolívar in Mompox, Colombia

Simón Bolívar

Simón Bolívar (1783–1830) was one of South America's greatest heroes and a very **powerful** man. In Spanish, Simón Bolívar is often called *El Libertador*, which means "The Liberator[1]." Spanish is the national language in at least 22 countries. This name is a very good one because he helped six countries become independent from Spain: Bolivia (1809), Colombia (1819), Ecuador (1820), Panama (1821), Peru (1821), and his home country of Venezuela (1811). In fact, Bolivia is named for Bolívar. Not many people have countries named after them. Because these six countries together are **approximately** the same size as modern Europe, their independence was an important event in history. Although Bolívar's name is not as well-known outside Latin America, many people there believe that he is the most important person in their history.

[1]liberator: someone who helps others become free

1. What is the main idea of the paragraph? _____

   _____

2. Does the paragraph have a topic sentence? If so, write it here. If not, write one here.

   _____

3. Are all the sentences related to the topic? _____ If not, cross out the unrelated sentence(s).

4. What is the concluding sentence? Write it here.

   _____

   _____

Mechanics: Capitalization and End Punctuation

A **capital letter** indicates that the word is at the beginning of a sentence or is a name. Names are given to a specific person (**Dr.** **J**enkins), a place (**J**apan), a company (**S**wiss **A**irlines), and a variety of other things (**H**ello **K**itty, the **U**nited **N**ations,...).

End punctuation includes periods (.), question marks (?), and exclamation marks (!).

For more information, see "Capitalization and Punctuation" in the *Writer's Handbook*.

ACTIVITY 10 | Editing capitalization and end punctuation

Each sentence has (x) number of errors. Find and correct them.

1. the geography of turkey is unique. (3)

2. most countries are on one continent, but turkey lies in both asia and Europe (4)

3. the asian part of the Country is much larger than the european part (5)

4. two european countries that border turkey are bulgaria and Greece (5)

5. turkey has coasts on the mediterranean sea and the black sea. (5)

6. half of it's land is higher than 1,000 meters above sea level (3)

7. in fact, two-thirds of the country is higher than 800 meters above sea level (2)

8. the geography is one reason millions of tourists visit this country every year (2)

ACTIVITY 11 | Copying a paragraph

On a separate piece of paper, write the corrected sentences from Activity 10 in paragraph form. Do not change the order. Make sure you indent your paragraph and correct all errors in capitalization and end punctuation. Write a title on the top line.

The Bosphorus Bridge in Istanbul, Turkey, connects Asia and Europe.

23

Grammar: Subject-Verb Agreement in the Simple Present

EXPLANATION	EXAMPLES
Make sure the verb form matches the subject in number. If the subject is singular, the verb should be singular. If the subject is plural, the verb should be plural. Remember to use the -s form of the verb with *he, she,* and *it.*	Singular: A good student **learns** new words every day. Plural: Good students **learn** new words every day.
Prepositional phrases include a preposition (*at, for, by, with, without, in, of,* and so on.) + an object of the preposition (a noun, noun phrase, pronoun). The object of a preposition is never the subject.	The main **products** of Brazil and Colombia **are** coffee and aluminum. The main **product** of Brazil and Colombia **is** coffee.
The noun after *there is* or *there are* is the subject of the sentence.	There **is a dictionary** on the table. There **are three reasons** for this decision.
Pronouns with *every-, some-,* or *any-* are always singular. Nouns with *each* or *every* are also singular.	**Everyone has** an accent of some kind. **Every** student **needs** a book and a workbook.
Gerunds (*-ing* words used as a noun) are always singular.	**Drinking** milk **is** good for your body. **Drinking** milk and juice **is** good for your body.

ACTIVITY 12 | Editing subject-verb agreement errors

Read the sentences. If the sentence is correct, write *C.* If it is incorrect, write *I* and correct it. There are six sentences with errors.

1. ___I___ The main method of transportation in these five islands ~~are~~ *is* the public bus system.

2. _____ Everybody prefers to live near the ocean because it is less dry.

3. _____ The trees behind the new high school is very tall.

4. _____ Earth revolves around the sun.

5. _____ According to the new rules, a pilot and a copilot flies this type of large plane.

6. _____ The three baby elephants at the zoo weighs just under 300 pounds.

7. _____ There are many interesting things to do in San Francisco.

8. _____ Each player on both teams need the ability to run very fast.

9. _____ Laughing with friends is a healthy way to spend time.

10. _____ Everyone with five correct answers get a passing grade.

ACTIVITY 13 | Practicing subject-verb agreement

Choose the correct verb form in each sentence.

1. One reason many people want to visit Asia **(is / are)** to see Japan.

2. In many people's opinions, the best places to visit in Japan **(is / are)** Tokyo and Kyoto.

3. Tokyo **(is / are)** a very modern city with many tall buildings.

4. In fact, the skyscrapers in Tokyo **(is / are)** some of the tallest buildings in the world.

5. However, the city skyline with these incredibly tall buildings **(do / does)** not look like the scenery in Kyoto at all.

6. Life in Kyoto **(move / moves)** more slowly than life in Tokyo.

7. Kyoto **(is / are)** not only smaller but also much older.

8. Kyoto **(was / were)** the capital of Japan a long time ago.

9. There **(is / are)** still many historic buildings in Kyoto, so tourists can see them all over the city.

10. Life in these two places **(is / are)** quite different, and tourists **(visit / visits)** each city for very different reasons.

ACTIVITY 14 | Copying a paragraph

Copy the sentences from Activity 13 in the same order on a separate piece of paper. Make sure your paragraph is indented. Write a title.

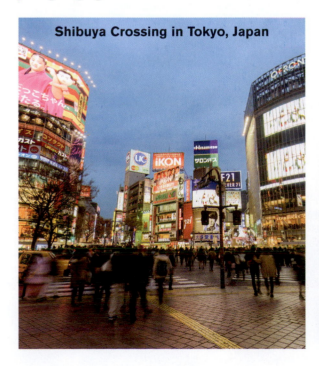

Shibuya Crossing in Tokyo, Japan

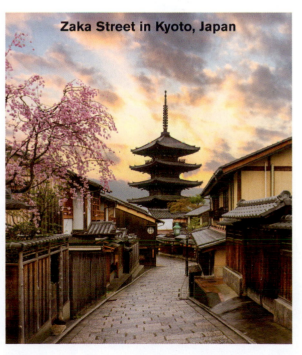

Zaka Street in Kyoto, Japan

ACTIVITY 15 | Correcting subject-verb agreement errors

Read the paragraph. It has seven errors in subject-verb agreement. Cross out each error and write the correct form above it.

> **WORDS TO KNOW** Paragraph 1.7
>
> **a great deal (of):** (phr) a lot of; a large amount
> **extremely:** (adv) very
>
> **patient:** (adj) calm; having the ability to wait calmly

PARAGRAPH 1.7

The Hard Work of a Kindergarten Teacher

Some people think that Mira Ahmed has an easy job, but teaching a class of 22 very young children ~~are~~ *is* not easy. Mira is a kindergarten teacher. Class begins at 8:00 a.m., but every teacher arrive by 7:30. Before class, Mira set up the room for her students. The students arrive between 7:45 and 8:00, and then the class begins. The young students in her class keeps her **extremely** busy for the rest of the day. They play games and learn new things. However, there is always a few small problems. Sometimes a child runs around the room or cry, but Mira tries to be very **patient** with all of her students. After school, she attends meetings and prepare lessons for the next day. Mira says she loves her job, but it really is **a great deal** of work.

Young students take part in classes at a primary school in Abu Dhabi, UAE.

BUILDING BETTER VOCABULARY

WORDS TO KNOW

a great deal (of) (phr)	convince (v) **AW**	population (n)
allow (v)	differ (v)	powerful (adj)
approximately (adv) **AW**	divided (adj)	remove (v) **AW**
at least (phr)	extremely (adv)	require (v) **AW**
attraction (n)	ingredient (n)	take care of (phr v)
boil (v)	majority (n) **AW**	take place (v phr)
contrast (n) **AW**	obvious (adj) **AW**	take up (phr v)
convenient (adj)	patient (adj)	traditional (adj) **AW**

AW This icon indicates that the word is on an academic word list.

ACTIVITY 16 | Word associations

Circle the word or phrase that is more closely related to the bold word on the left.

1. allow	let	put
2. attraction	popular place	young animal
3. boil	very difficult people	very hot water
4. contrast	similarities	differences
5. convenient	easy	free
6. ingredients	for a recipe	for a suitcase
7. majority	less than half	more than half
8. population	money	people
9. remove	subtract	add
10. require	give	need

ACTIVITY 17 | Collocations

Fill in the blank with the word or phrase that most naturally completes the phrase.

at least	attraction	deal of	extremely	patient

1. a great _____ money

2. _____ two people

3. a tourist _____

4. a _____ teacher

5. _____ important

approximately	convenient	convince	obvious	powerful

6. an _____ error

7. at _____ 2 p.m.

8. a _____ location

9. _____ someone

10. a _____ earthquake

ACTIVITY 18 | Word forms

Complete each sentence with the correct word form. Use the correct forms of the words.

NOUN	VERB	ADJECTIVE	ADVERB	SENTENCES
attraction	attract	attractive		**1.** The local beaches _____ a lot of tourists in spring and fall.
difference	differ	different	differently	**2.** The words *father* and *feather* _____ by only one letter: *e*. **3.** What is the _____ between the two ideas? **4.** Purple and violet look similar to us, but to artists, these colors are very _____.
division	divide	divided		**5.** In Ms. Valencia's math lessons, students learn how to add, subtract, multiply, and _____.
requirement	require	required		**6.** Most airlines _____ a paid ticket for a child over two years old. **7.** One of the _____ of being a babysitter is to know how to get help in an emergency.
tradition		traditional	traditionally	**8.** Spain has an interesting New Year's _____: at midnight, people eat 12 grapes.

ACTIVITY 19 | Vocabulary in writing

Choose five words from Words to Know. Write a complete sentence with each word.

1. _____

2. _____

3. _____

4. _____

5. _____

BUILDING BETTER SENTENCES

ACTIVITY 20 | Editing

Each sentence has two errors. Find and correct them.

1. Many politicians in this country believes the law will to change in the near future.

2. Cell phones are advanced than they was in the past.

3. The normal retirement age for a teacher in the U.K. is 60, some teachers retire when they have 55 years old.

4. What was the political and economic effects of the great Wall of China?

5. A word that end in -*ing* can be a noun, a verb, or a adjective.

ACTIVITY 21 | Writing sentences

Read the pairs of words. Write an original sentence using the words listed.

1. (take up/space) _His desk takes up a lot of space in his office._

2. (ingredient/recipe) _____

_____

3. (patient/driver) _____

_____

4. (population/Canada) _____

_____

5. (take care of/problem) _____

_____

6. (require/credit card) _____

_____

Combining Sentences

Some writers like to keep their sentences short. They believe they will make mistakes if they write longer, more difficult sentences. However, longer sentences connect ideas, and this makes it easier for the reader to understand. The most important information from each sentence can be used to create longer and smoother sentences.

A word or word form may change or be omitted, but no ideas are changed or omitted. Remember that there is usually more than one way to combine sentences. Study these sentences. The important information is circled.

There was a (storm) (yesterday.)

It was (strong.)

It moved (quickly) (toward the city.)

Now read these longer, smoother sentences:

Yesterday, a strong storm moved quickly toward the city.

There was a strong storm that moved quickly toward the city yesterday.

ACTIVITY 22 | Combining sentences

Combine the ideas into one sentence. You may change the word forms, but do not change or omit any ideas. There may be more than one answer.

1. The weather was extremely cold yesterday.
A majority of the flights departed late.
The flights were from Boston.

_____

_____

2. Jim Thorpe won medals.
The medals were Olympic medals.
They were gold medals.
He won them in 1912.
He was not allowed to keep the medals..

_____

_____

3. Thailand is a country in Southeast Asia.
Malaysia is a country in Southeast Asia.
Thailand is interesting, and Malaysia is, too.
Very few tourists from North or South America visit Malaysia or Thailand.

WRITING

ACTIVITY 23 | Writing a paragraph

Write a paragraph. Follow these guidelines.

1. Complete the chart. Then choose the topic and topic sentence you like best.

2. Indent the first line and write the topic sentence.

3. Write five to twelve related sentences.

4. Write a concluding sentence.

5. Use at least two of the vocabulary words or phrases from Words to Know. Underline them.

TOPIC	TOPIC SENTENCE
Color	• In different cultures, the meaning of a color can vary a great deal. • Colors can affect the way you feel.
Food	• Three healthy snacks are _____ • The easiest food to prepare is _____
People	• A _____ (job title) has a very difficult job. • If I could meet anyone in history, I would like to meet _____ .

Chefchaouen, Morocco,
where they say the color
blue represents the sky and
heavens; some say it helps
keep mosquitoes away.

Peer Editing

Peer Editing is when your classmates (your peers) read your paper and make comments using a set of questions and guidelines. You will read someone else's paper, too. Peer editing can help you strengthen any areas in your paragraph that are weak or that appear confusing to the reader.

This is what usually happens in peer editing:

1. A peer reads your writing.
2. Your peer gives you suggestions and ideas for making your writing better.
3. You listen carefully to what your peer says.
4. You think about making the changes your peer suggests. If the comments are negative, remember that the comments are about the mistakes in your writing, not about you.

Peer Editing Comments

When you peer edit a classmate's writing, choose your words carefully. Make sure that:

- Your comments are helpful. Be specific about the mistakes.

  Helpful: "You forgot to put the word *at* here."
  Not helpful: "This is incorrect."

- Your comments are polite. Say things the way you would want someone to tell you.

  Polite: "What does this sentence mean? Can you make the meaning clearer?"
  Not polite: "What is this? It doesn't make any sense at all!"

Before you write a comment, ask yourself, "Will this be helpful to the writer? Would I want someone to tell me this?"

WRITER'S NOTE Read, Read, Read!

It is important for you to understand why a piece of writing is good or is not good, and the best way to do this is to read books, newspapers, and other texts as often as you can. The more writing styles you become familiar with, the better your writing will be.

ACTIVITY 24 | Peer editing

Work with a partner. Read your partner's paragraph from Activity 23. Use Peer Editing Form 1 in the *Writer's Handbook*. Offer positive suggestions to help your partner write a better paragraph. Consider your partner's comments as you revise your paragraph.

Additional Topics for Writing

Here are more ideas for writing a paragraph. When you write your paragraph, follow the guidelines in Activity 23.

TOPIC 1: Look at the photo at the beginning of the unit. Write about your hometown or a place you know well. How is it similar to Rio de Janerio? How is it different? Compare the two places.

TOPIC 2: Write about your bedroom. What does it look like? What things does it have in it?

TOPIC 3: Write about a famous living person. What does this person do? Why is he/she famous?

TOPIC 4: Which is more difficult to learn: English or your language? What parts of the language do you find hard? Can you give suggestions for someone learning the language?

TOPIC 5: Write about your favorite season. What do you do during this season? How does it make you feel?

TEST PREP

You should spend about 25 minutes on this task. Write a paragraph with six to ten sentences about the following topic.

Is being a tour guide a good job? How is it easy or difficult? What kinds of things does a tour guide do every day?

TIP

Take five minutes to plan before you start writing. First, list all the ideas you have about the topic. Then think about which ideas have the best supporting examples or ideas. Identify your main idea. Then write a topic sentence that represents your best ideas.

Give reasons for your opinion and include any relevant examples from your knowledge or experience. Remember to use the simple present and check for correct subject-verb agreement. Check for correct capitalization and end punctuation. Write at least 150 words.

2 | Developing Ideas for Writing

OBJECTIVES
- Brainstorm ideas for writing
- Identify and write simple and compound sentences
- Use descriptive adjectives
- Write effective titles
- Write a paragraph

a lightning storm at night over the Grand Canyon in Arizona, USA

FREEWRITE | Have you ever experienced a dangerous or frightenig storm? What did you do? How did you feel? Write five to ten sentences.

ELEMENTS OF GREAT WRITING

What Is Brainstorming?

How do writers find topics for their writing? One way is brainstorming.

Brainstorming is quickly writing down all the thoughts that come into your head. When you brainstorm, you do not think about whether an idea is good or bad or whether your writing is correct. You simply write your ideas as fast as you can. This is called brainstorming because it feels like there is a storm of ideas in your head.

For example, imagine there is a fire at your school right now. What should you do? Here are some ideas that someone might brainstorm. Do you have any other ideas you can add?

ACTIVITY 1 | Brainstorming practice

Read the situation. Then brainstorm ideas using the cluster diagram below. Your goal is to write as many ideas as you can in two minutes. Do not worry about being right or wrong.

Next Saturday is your grandmother's birthday. She is going to be 85 years old. What will you get for her? Make a list of five suitable birthday gifts for her on this special day.

Brainstorming Ideas with Others

Sometimes it is helpful to work with other writers and share ideas. Remember that in brainstorming, there are no bad ideas. The purpose of brainstorming is to produce as many ideas as possible. The advantage of group brainstorming is that you have more ideas and you also get some immediate feedback as people react to each new idea.

ACTIVITY 2 | Group brainstorming practice

Work in a group. Compare your ideas from Activity 1. Write your group's three best ideas.

1. _____

2. _____

3. _____

ACTIVITY 3 | Writing about your ideas

Complete the sentences with information about your group's three best ideas.

1. Our group thinks the best gift is _____

   because _____.

2. Our second idea is _____

   because _____.

3. Our third suggestion is _____

   because _____.

ACTIVITY 4 | Presenting your group's ideas

With your group, follow these steps to prepare a presentation of your gift ideas.

1. Prepare five slides (or choose another way to present).

   Slide 1: Give the title of your slide show. Include the names of your group members.

   Slides 2, 3, and 4: Prepare one slide for each of your three ideas. What is the idea? You may want to add some short phrases to catch the audience's attention.

   Slide 5: Explain why your three ideas are perfect for this occasion.

2. Present your group's ideas to the whole class. After all of the presentations, talk about the pros and cons of some of the ideas. As a class, choose the best one or two ideas.

How Brainstorming Works

A good writer brainstorms a topic by completing these two important steps:

1. thinking about the topic
2. quickly writing down words and ideas

Some writers use cluster diagrams to connect their ideas. Look at this example, which shows brainstorming for Paragraph 1.1, "Chile and Brazil." You can see that the writer wrote many ideas and crossed out some of them. There are several ideas that are not in the final paragraph. In addition, a few ideas in the final paragraph are not in the diagram.

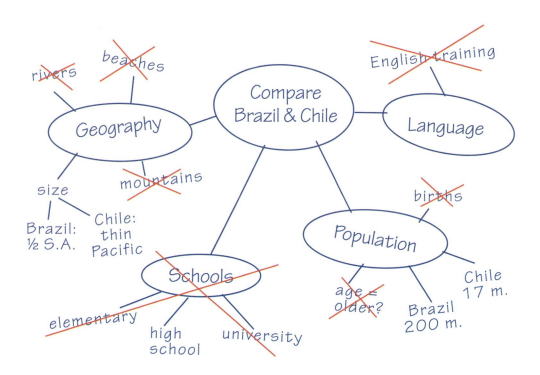

ACTIVITY 5 | Brainstorming practice

Follow these steps to brainstorm a paragraph about dangerous weather situations.

1. Think of a few dangerous weather situations. What are three things a person should do in each kind of weather? Brainstorm ideas in your notebook. Use a cluster diagram.

2. Circle the ideas that you think are the best ones to include in a paragraph.

3. Compare and discuss your ideas with a partner. When you compare your notes, be prepared to say why you want to keep some ideas and why you want to take out others. Decide which weather situation is best to write about. What information will be in the final paragraph? Share your decisions with the class.

Grammar: Descriptive Adjectives

EXPLANATION	EXAMPLES
Descriptive adjectives are important in writing. They give more detail about nouns and make your writing more interesting. They also help your reader understand your ideas more clearly.	The graduation speech was really **great**. Better: The graduation speech was **powerful**. The graduation speech was **outstanding**.
In a sentence, descriptive adjectives can appear in two places: • before a noun • after linking verbs like *be* and *seem*	An alligator is a **dangerous** <u>animal</u>. **Confusing** <u>words</u> like *make* and *do* cause problems for students. In Iraq, it <u>is</u> very **hot** in July. Many students <u>seemed</u> **surprised** when the teacher gave the test.

ACTIVITY 6 | Editing descriptive adjectives

Circle the two descriptive adjectives in each sentence. Correct any errors you see in the location of the adjectives by drawing an arrow to the correct place.

1. This website has information (important) about (fresh) food.

2. The pyramids in Egypt are examples excellent of ancient architecture.

3. In Alaska, summer days are very long.

4. A new computer can do this work difficult very quickly.

5. Colorado is a place fabulous to go skiing when it is cold.

6. Giraffes have very long necks and are the tallest mammals on Earth.

7. In 1891, a Canadian coach invented the game of basketball because he wanted a sport that was less dangerous than football.

8. Coffee is one of Vietnam's exports main, which is surprising to many people.

9. The earthquake violent caused frightening aftershocks for several days.

10. The clever detective discovered that the husband jealous started the fire.

11. A safe place to hide during a tornado is in an underground room such as a basement.

12. Alligators are fast even though their legs are very short.

ACTIVITY 7 | Using descriptive adjectives in a paragraph

Complete Paragraph 2.1 with the adjectives in the box below Words to Know. Use the context to determine the best word.

> **WORDS TO KNOW** Paragraph 2.1
>
> **ancient:** (adj) very old
> **highly:** (adv) very much; strongly
> **major:** (adj) main; most important
>
> **odd:** (adj) strange or unusual
> **peaceful:** (adj) calm; quiet
> **recommend:** (v) to tell others about something you like

busy	loud	**major**	**odd**
cool	lucky	modern	**peaceful**

PARAGRAPH 2.1

The Sights and Sounds of the Chao Phraya River

On our trip to Bangkok , Thailand, my friends and I took a boat trip at sunset on the Chao Phraya River, which is one of the [1]_____ rivers in Thailand. This river is very [2]_____, with many water taxis, fishing boats, and tourist boats. Bangkok residents use these boats every day because they are faster than driving a car. The traffic on Bangkok's streets is worse than it is on the river. Our boat was crowded, but we flew down the river, enjoying the [3]_____ breeze. We saw many tall buildings and [4]_____ hotels, which were [5]_____ to see next to the **ancient** palaces and temples. The city streets are [6]_____ because of the noise from so many cars, but the river is [7]_____. If you are [8]_____ enough to travel to Bangkok, I **highly recommend** taking a boat trip along the Chao Phraya River.

The Chao Phraya River at sunset, Bangkok, Thailand

Adjectives with More Exact Meanings

When you write, it is important to use words that have the exact meaning that you want. Sometimes English has two or more adjectives with similar meanings, but one adjective might be positive while the other is negative. Or one might be casual and the other formal. Knowing a variety of similar adjectives with slightly different meanings will make your writing more interesting and more precise.

For example, the basic meanings of the words *thrifty* and *stingy* are similar—they both describe someone who is careful with money. However, there is a big difference in the feeling these words give to the reader or listener. The *thrifty* person is smart with money while the *stingy* person is greedy and does not want to spend money. Being thrifty is good while being stingy is not.

WRITER'S NOTE Using a Thesaurus

Use a thesaurus to find synonyms (*syn.*) and antonyms (*ant.*) of words. For example, instead of saying a *"great"* gift, find a word to replace *great*. Remember to find the correct meaning for any word. The blue highlighted definitions are the correct ones for this context.

great 1 immense, enormous. *Ant.* small. **2** famous, distinguished. *Ant.* unknown. **3** marvelous, splendid, first-rate. *Ant.* weak. **4** outstanding, fantastic | cool, awesome.

ACTIVITY 8 | Using more exact adjectives

Use a thesaurus to find positive and negative adjectives to complete the phrases. Do not use simple words, such as *nice* or *bad*.

POSITIVE	NEGATIVE
1. a/an _____ gift	a/an _____ gift
2. a/an _____ idea	a/an _____ idea
3. a/an _____ result	a/an _____ result
4. this _____ reason	this _____ reason
5. one of the _____ solutions	one of the _____ solutions
6. a _____ river	a _____ river

ACTIVITY 9 | Recognizing positive and negative adjectives

Read Paragraphs 2.2 and 2.3. Underline the descriptive adjectives in each. There are 11 in Paragraph 2.2 and 8 in Paragraph 2.3. Then discuss with a partner which adjectives are positive and which are negative.

> **WORDS TO KNOW** Paragraphs 2.2 to 2.3
>
> **abundant:** (adj) more than enough
> **affect:** (v) to produce a change
> **limited:** (adj) not many; not much
> **polluted:** (adj) unclean; contaminated
>
> **provide:** (v) to supply, give
> **quality:** (n) how good something is
> **shade:** (n) an area with no sunlight
> **supply:** (n) an amount

PARAGRAPH 2.2

River A is an <u>important</u> part of the forest, and the **quality** of the river **affects** the environment around it. The fresh, clear water is home to a wide variety of fish and plants. The fish enjoy the **abundant supply** of insects near the beautiful river. The tall trees near the river are green and healthy. Wild animals come to drink the cool water and rest in the **shade** of the trees along the river.

PARAGRAPH 2.3

River B is an <u>important</u> part of the forest, and the quality of the river affects the environment around it. The slow, brown water does not contain fish or plants. The fish fight to catch the very **limited** number of insects that live near the dirty river. The old trees near the river are dying. They do not **provide** enough cover for the wild animals that try to drink from the **polluted** river.

ACTIVITY 10 | Completing sentences with descriptive adjectives

Add descriptive adjectives to complete each sentence. Do not use any adjective more than once. Then compare answers with your classmates.

1. The most _____ reason for getting a university degree is to be able to get a(n) _____ job in the future.

2. A(n) _____ spider scared my _____ brother.

3. In this picture, three _____ cows are eating grass on the _____ mountain.

4. A _____ driver avoids _____ situations by being very _____ at all times when driving.

5. Unfortunately, a new snack food will not sell well if it is not _____ and _____ .

6. The food in Italy is _____ because it has various kinds of pasta and _____ sauces.

7. Dogs are _____ animals with a(n) _____ ability to improve the lives of _____ people.

8. The water at the beach was _____ , and the swimmers were _____ .

ACTIVITY 11 | Changing meaning with descriptive adjectives

The paragraph describes a man walking into a room. Decide whether you want your reader to see a positive or negative image of this person. Add adjectives to complete the paragraph. Add a title to the top line. Use a dictionary or thesaurus to help you.

_____

A [1]_____ man entered the [2]_____ party. He had [3]_____ hair and wore [4]_____ clothing. The shoes he wore were very [5]_____ . The man was not [6]_____ . Everyone in the room was [7]_____ when they first saw him. He was a(n) [8]_____ man, too. At first, the man seemed [9]_____ , but then he became more [10]_____ . He was actually very [11]_____ . The man soon left and everyone was [12]_____ that they met him.

Grammar: Simple vs. Compound Sentences

Simple sentences usually have one subject and one verb. In other words, they have one independent clause. An **independent clause** has one subject-verb relationship, and it can stand alone as a sentence. Sometimes a simple sentence has more than one subject or verb, but it never has more than one clause.

SIMPLE SENTENCES	
SUBJECT(S)	VERB(S) + OTHER INFORMATION
Chile	**imports** oil from Brazil.
Chile	**imports** oil and **exports** copper.
Chile and **Brazil**	**import** clothing from China.
Chile and **Brazil**	**import** clothing and **export** copper.

Compound sentences are usually made of two simple sentences (independent clauses). Compound sentences need a coordinating conjunction (*and, but, or, so*) to connect the two sentences. Use a comma before the connecting word in a compound sentence.

COMPOUND SENTENCES		
INDEPENDENT CLAUSE 1	CONJ	INDEPENDENT CLAUSE 2
Chile exports copper,	**and**	**Brazil exports** sugar.
Chile has a very long seacoast,	**so**	**fishing is** a big business there.
Chile is an extremely long country,	**but**	**it is** not wide at all.
Tourists can visit the pyramids,	**or**	**they can relax** on a beach.

If both sentences have a noun that names the same person, place, or thing, replace the second noun with a pronoun. Do not repeat the noun.

> **Tourists** can visit the pyramids, or **they** can relax on a beach.

ACTIVITY 12 | Identifying sentence types

For each sentence, underline the subject(s) and circle the verb(s). Then write *S* if it is a simple sentence or *C* if it is a compound sentence. Add a comma in the compound sentences.

_____ **1.** Confusing words such as the verbs *make* and *do* may cause problems for some students.

_____ **2.** This process feels like a storm of ideas in your mind so it is called "brainstorming."

_____ **3.** Certain words in a title may catch the reader's attention but some titles are too general and do not create interest.

_____ **4.** An independent clause has one subject-verb relationship and it can stand alone as a sentence.

_____ **5.** All of the sentences in a well-written paragraph talk about one topic.

_____ **6.** The Statue of Liberty weighs 450,000 pounds (204,117 kilograms) and it is 152 feet (46 meters) high.

_____ **7.** Unlike in previous years, the slow, brown water in the Galona River today does not contain fish or plants.

_____ **8.** Sometimes a simple sentence has a compound subject or verb but it never has more than one clause.

ACTIVITY 13 | Identifying sentence types

For each sentence in the paragraph, underline the subject(s) and circle the main verb(s). Add a comma in the compound sentences.

PARAGRAPH 2.4

A Visit to New York City

Each year, millions of excited tourists from the United States and other countries all over the world travel to New York City. About 80 percent of these visitors come from the United States and about 20 percent come from other countries. These tourists come to see the bright lights and exciting life of New York City. Two of the most popular destinations for tourists in New York are the Empire State Building and the Statue of Liberty. Perhaps one of the most interesting and most amazing things to see is Central Park. Many tourists start their New York City experience by visiting Times Square. Some tourists want to go on tours through companies but other tourists prefer to discover the city on their own. New York City has many things to see and do so millions of people visit the city each year.

35

ACTIVITY 14 | Analyzing compound sentences

For each sentence, underline the subject(s) and circle the main verb(s). Then add a comma.

> **WORDS TO KNOW** Activity 14
>
> **area:** (n) a general place
> **assistance:** (n) help
> **contract:** (n) a business agreement in writing
> **customer:** (n) a person who buys things
> **fee:** (n) a payment for services
>
> **final:** (adj) the last
> **function:** (v) to work
> **location:** (n) a place
> **section:** (n) a part
> **similar:** (adj) like

1. The **location** of the city is near the ocean but the weather in this **area** can be very dry.

2. Last year's **contract** was not easy to understand and the new contract is **similar**.

3. The first **section** of the **final** exam asks questions about the War of 1812 and it will take about 20 minutes to answer well.

4. Some **customers** want a great deal of **assistance** when making a purchase but others prefer to **function** independently.

5. People do not understand how to pay late **fees** so the instructions are on the website.

ACTIVITY 15 | Writing compound sentences

Complete each compound sentence. Be sure to add a comma in the correct location.

1. Washington, DC, is the capital of the country but _____

_____

2. Fast food is very cheap so _____

_____

3. Learning new vocabulary is important and _____

_____

4. Some students have a part-time job and _____

_____

5. September has 30 days so _____

_____

Titles

A **title** tells you what you will find in a book, a movie, a story, or a text. A title is not usually a sentence. A title is usually very short. Sometimes the title is only one word, such as the movie titles *Spiderman, Batman,* or *Titanic.*

A good title has something that catches the reader's interest, but it does not tell everything about the paragraph. For example, imagine that you wrote a paragraph about why it is difficult to write well in English. Consider these possible titles for this paragraph:

TITLE	COMMENT
English Is Difficult	✗ A title is not usually a sentence.
A Difficult Task	✗ The word *task* may interest the reader, but this title is still too general.
Difficulties in English	✗ The word *difficulties* catches the reader's attention. The word *English* tells us what kind of difficulties, but there is no mention of *writing*. This paragraph is about writing in English.
Challenges with Writing in English	✔ This title uses the word *challenges*, which attracts readers' attention. The title also mentions *writing* and *English*, so the reader knows exactly what to expect from the paragraph.

ACTIVITY 16 | Choosing a good title

Read the three titles and check (✓) the best one.

1. _____ Do Not Get a Cat for a Pet
_____ Problems with Having a Pet Cat
_____ I Will Never Have a Cat Again

2. _____ How to Buy a Used Car
_____ Buying a Used Car Can Be a Problem
_____ Cars

3. _____ Halloween Is Fun for Kids
_____ Halloween, Fun, and Kids
_____ The Best Holiday for Kids

4. _____ Popcorn Is Good for Our Health
_____ The Health Benefits of Popcorn
_____ Healthy Times for Popcorn

5. _____ Learning to Use U.S. Money
_____ A Dime Is Smaller Than a Penny
_____ Pennies, Nickels, Dimes, Quarters

6. _____ Three Good Websites for Cheap Travel
_____ I Prefer These Three Websites
_____ Best Website

7. _____ Meat Is Bad for Humans
_____ A Vegetarian Breakfast and Lunch
_____ Benefits of a Vegetarian Diet

8. _____ Two Fast-Food Meals
_____ Fast Food
_____ Cheeseburgers: Taste Better Than Fried Chicken

BUILDING BETTER VOCABULARY

WORDS TO KNOW

abundant (adj)	final (adj) AW	polluted (adj)
affect (v) AW	function (v) AW	provide (v)
ancient (adj)	highly (adv)	quality (n)
area (n) AW	limited (adj)	recommend (v)
assistance (n) AW	location (n) AW	section (n) AW
contract (n) AW	major (adj) AW	shade (n)
customer (n)	odd (adj) AW	similar (adj) AW
fee (n) AW	peaceful (adj)	supply (n)

ACTIVITY 17 | Word associations

Circle the word or phrase that is more closely related to the bold word on the left.

1. assistance	food	help
2. ancient	new	old
3. customers	buyers	drivers
4. final	first	last
5. function	listen	work
6. highly	never	very
7. location	where	why
8. odd	unhappy	unusual
9. provide	give	learn
10. shade	no money	no light

ACTIVITY 18 | Collocations

Fill in the blank with the word that most naturally completes the phrase.

affect	function	recommend	section	similar

1. to _____ a good restaurant

2. to _____ well

3. the children's _____ in a bookstore

4. a website _____ to YouTube

5. to _____ your health

| contract | fees | major | polluted | provide |

6. to _____ help to someone

7. a _____ between two businesses

8. very high _____

9. a _____ lake

10. a _____ problem

ACTIVITY 19 | Word forms

Complete each sentence with the correct word form. Use the correct forms of the words.

NOUN	VERB	ADJECTIVE	ADVERB	SENTENCES
abundance		abundant	abundantly	**1.** This city has an _____ supply of fresh water.
function	function	functional	functionally	**2.** Use this diagram to explain the _____ of the heart. **3.** How does this machine _____?
limit	limit	limited		**4.** The speed _____ has increased in many states. **5** Students must _____ their presentations to 20 minutes.
pollution	pollute	polluted		**6.** Air _____ is a severe problem in some countries.
recommendation	recommend	recommended		**7.** A doctor can _____ a different type of medicine. **8.** The _____ amount of medicine is one tablespoon.
similarity		similar	similarly	**9.** Portuguese is _____ to Spanish and French. **10.** Explain the _____ between baseball and cricket.

ACTIVITY 20 | Vocabulary in writing

Choose five words from Words to Know. Write a compound sentence with each word.
Use commas in the correct place.

1. _____

   _____

2. _____

   _____

3. _____

   _____

4. _____

   _____

5. _____

   _____

BUILDING BETTER SENTENCES

ACTIVITY 21 | Writing descriptive sentences

Write an original compound sentence with the nouns listed. Include at least one descriptive
adjective in each sentence. Circle the descriptive adjectives.

1. (vacation/California) *California is a (wonderful) place for a vacation, but Hawaii is better.*

2. (students/computers) _____

   _____

3. (dictionaries/libraries) _____

   _____

4. (trees/forest) _____

   _____

5. (skyscraper/city) _____

   _____

Looking up at the old Chicago Water Tower and modern skyscrapers

ACTIVITY 22 | Combining sentences

Combine the ideas into one sentence. You may change the word forms, but do not change or omit any ideas. There may be more than one answer.

1. Chicago is a city.
Chicago is modern.
Chicago has many buildings.
The buildings in Chicago are tall.
Chicago has beautiful architecture.

_____

_____

2. Writers should make a list.
This is a list of ideas.
The ideas are important.
The ideas are also interesting.
Writers should do this before they begin writing.
These writers are serious.

_____

_____

3. Wood is a resource.
This resource is natural.
This resource is abundant.
This resource is in Canada.

_____

_____

WRITING

ACTIVITY 23 | Brainstorming and writing a paragraph

Write a paragraph. Follow these guidelines.

1. Choose one of these topics: sports, technology, or vacations. Use the cluster diagram to brainstorm a possible paragraph about the topic. Put the main topic in the center and ideas about it in the outer circles. You can add more supporting information around each circle.

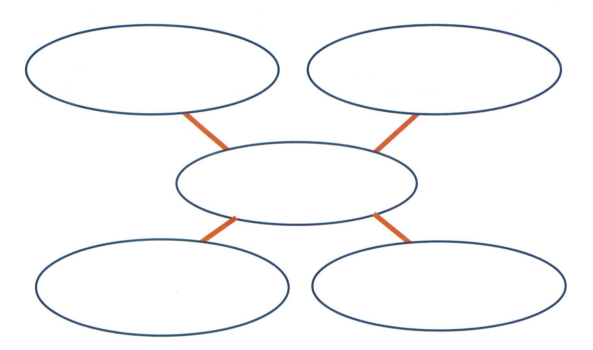

2. Look at your ideas and cross out the ones that you do not think will work.

3. Use the ideas that you brainstormed to create sentences for your paragraph. Write a paragraph with five to ten sentences on a separate piece of paper. Include at least two compound sentences. Use commas correctly.

4. Include the four features of a good paragraph.

   ☐ Is the first line of the paragraph indented?
   ☐ Does the paragraph have a topic sentence that states the main idea?
   ☐ Are all of the sentences in the paragraph about the topic?
   ☐ Does the paragraph have a concluding sentence?

5. Give your paragraph a title.

6. Use at least two of the vocabulary words or phrases presented in the Words to Know box.

7. Be sure to proofread. Check for subject-verb agreement and use a variety of descriptive adjectives.

ACTIVITY 24 | Peer editing

Work with a partner. Read your partner's paragraph from Activity 23. Use Peer Editing Form 2 in the *Writer's Handbook*. Offer positive suggestions to help your partner write a better paragraph. Consider your partner's comments as you revise your paragraph.

Additional Topics for Writing

Here are more ideas for writing a paragraph. When you write your paragraph, follow the guidelines in Activity 23.

TOPIC 1: Look at the photo at the beginning of the unit. Describe a dangerous weather event you were in or know about. What happened? When was it? How did you feel?

TOPIC 2: Describe what you like to do on a fun night out (maybe dinner, a movie, or a trip to some other place).

TOPIC 3: Write about two things, people, or places. When you compare them, tell how they are similar or how they are different.

TOPIC 4: Write about ways that people can save money.

TOPIC 5: Write about three things that might be different 20 years from now. Do you think these things will be better or worse? Why?

TEST PREP

You should spend about 25 minutes on this task. Write a paragraph with six to ten sentences.

In your opinion, is English easy or difficult to learn?

Give reasons for your opinion and include any relevant examples from your knowledge or experience. Remember to use correct subject-verb agreement and descriptive adjectives. Write at least 150 words.

TIP

Leave time to review your writing. First, check that your ideas are clear and all relate to the topic sentence. Then proofread your paragraph and check for subject-verb agreement, correct use of commas, and correct end punctuation.

3 | Topic Sentences

Young boys play basketball after school in Havana, Cuba.

FREEWRITE   Look at the photo and write a story about one or all of the boys. Use your

ELEMENTS OF GREAT WRITING

What Is a Topic Sentence?

A **topic sentence** states the main idea of a paragraph. It is usually found at the beginning of a paragraph. A topic sentence has several important jobs. It:

- introduces the main idea
- limits or focuses the topic
- often tells the reader how the information will be organized in the paragraph

ACTIVITY 1 | Analyzing a paragraph

Discuss the questions. Then read the paragraph and answer the questions that follow.

1. Can you name three benefits of exercising regularly?
2. What are three reasons that people do not exercise regularly?

> **WORDS TO KNOW** Paragraph 3.1
>
> **climb:** (v) to go up   **in good shape:** (idiom) having good physical condition
> **improve:** (v) to make better   **reduce:** (v) to make less

PARAGRAPH 3.1

Reasons for Exercise

There are many excellent reasons for exercising several times each week. First, people who exercise look better. Exercise is important to keep our bodies **in good shape.** In addition, people who exercise have more energy. For example, a person who exercises can walk up stairs or **climb** hills more easily. People who exercise have a healthier heart, too. Finally, exercise **reduces** stress and helps you have a clear mind. Too much stress can cause you to worry a lot, and that is not good for your health. For these reasons, if you want to **improve** your health, you should exercise regularly.

An "anti-gravity" yoga class, where students use silk hammocks to lift themselves off the floor

1. What is the topic sentence? Write it here.

_____

_____

2. What do you expect to read about based on the topic sentence?

_____

_____

3. These words or expressions are very important to the organization of the paragraph. Number them in the same order that they are in the paragraph.

_____ finally   _____ first   _____ in addition   _____ for these reasons

4. Read the last sentence carefully. What do you think the purpose of this sentence is? Begin your answer with *The purpose of this sentence is to . . .*

_____

_____

ACTIVITY 2 | Recognizing good topic sentences

Read each set of sentences. Write the general topic that the sentences share. Then check (✓) the sentence you think is the best topic sentence. Discuss your reasons with the class.

1. General topic: winter	_____ Winter is a good season. _____ Winter weather is cold, and it snows. ✓ _____ The best season for children is winter.
2. General topic:	_____ Soccer is popular for many reasons. _____ For a soccer game, players need a special leather ball. _____ Soccer is a nice game.
3. General topic:	_____ There are many people in Los Angeles. _____ People from many different cultures live in Los Angeles. _____ Los Angeles is a big city in California.
4. General topic:	_____ Monolingual dictionaries have only one language, but bilingual dictionaries have two languages. _____ Many language students prefer bilingual dictionaries to monolingual dictionaries. _____ Dictionaries that have two languages, such as French and English, are called bilingual dictionaries.

Features of a Topic Sentence

A topic sentence has these important features.

1. **It has a controlling idea** that limits the topic and guides the flow of the paragraph. The controlling idea tells the reader what you will say about your topic. Here are two topic sentences. The topic is circled and the controlling idea is underlined.

   - (Soccer) is popular for many reasons.
     Explanation: The reader expects the paragraph to explain why soccer is popular.

   - Many (language students) prefer bilingual dictionaries to monolingual dictionaries.
     Explanation: The reader expects the paragraph to explain why this statement is true.

2. **It is not a fact.** For example, "Libraries have books" is not a good topic sentence. The information in this sentence is true, but it is a fact and there is little to say about it.

3. **It is specific.** "Tea is delicious" is not a good topic sentence because the information in the sentence is too general. If you want to write a paragraph about tea, make your topic sentence more specific, such as "Green tea has many health benefits."

4. **It is not _too_ specific.** "This dictionary contains more than 42,000 words" limits the topic too much. There is nothing else for the writer to say, so the paragraph cannot continue.

ACTIVITY 3 | Recognizing controlling ideas in topic sentences

Read each topic sentence. The topic is circled. Underline the controlling idea. What information do you expect to find in the paragraph? Share your answers with a partner.

WORDS TO KNOW Activity 3

addictive: (adj) having qualities that make you want to do something again and again
advantage: (n) a good or desirable quality or feature
confuse: (v) to mix up mentally so one cannot understand

educational: (adj) describes something that teaches or involves learning
investigator: (n) a person who tries to learn how something happened

---

1. (The new test) has three sections dealing with three important skills.

   Expectation: _____

   _____

2. The shocking (crash of the airplane) off the coast of Florida **confused investigators.**

   Expectation: _____

   _____

3. (Crossword puzzles) are not only **educational** and fun, but also **addictive.**

Expectation: _____

_____

4. Recent research has shown once again that (eating dark green, leafy vegetables) such as broccoli and cabbage may reduce the risk of some types of cancer.

Expectation: _____

_____

5. Although buying a house may seem like a good idea, (renting an apartment) has many **advantages.**

Expectation: _____

_____

ACTIVITY 4 | Recognizing good topic sentences and controlling ideas

Read the three sentences. Check (✓) the best topic sentence. Underline the controlling idea in that sentence. Be prepared to explain your selections.

WORDS TO KNOW Activity 4

contribution: (n) what someone does to help make something successful

immigrant: (n) someone who comes to live in a different country

recognize: (v) to give attention or notice to

---

1. _____ In an English class, most of the female students receive higher grades than the males.

_____ Research has shown female students like learning languages more than males do.

_____ Many students like languages very much.

2. _____ Cats are better pets than goldfish for many reasons.

_____ Cats and goldfish are both animals.

_____ Cats cannot swim very well, but goldfish can.

3. _____ The people in my office eat lunch from 11:30 to 12:30.

_____ Yesterday I went to work late, and my boss was of course very angry.

_____ Yesterday was the worst day of my life.

4. _____ Paul Cézanne was born in France in the last century.

_____ Paul Cézanne, the father of modern art, made important **contributions** to the history of art.

_____ Many of the museum visitors **recognized** Paul Cézanne's work immediately.

5. _____ Many Canadians speak French, and some of them speak Chinese.

_____ The current population of Canada includes **immigrants** from all over the world.

_____ A large number of new immigrants live in British Columbia, Canada, but not many of them speak German.

ACTIVITY 5 | Adding controlling ideas

These topic sentences are too general. Using the same topic, write a topic sentence with a clear controlling idea. Then compare your sentences with a partner's.

1. Flowers are beautiful.

Flowers are the best gift to receive when you are feeling down.

OR _Only four kinds of flowers grow during the short summers in Alaska._

2. Cats are nice. _____

_____

3. Paris is the capital of France. _____

_____

4. Reading blogs is interesting. _____

_____

5. Running is a hobby. _____

_____

ACTIVITY 6 | Studying the controlling idea of a paragraph

Answer the questions.

1. Write the topic sentence from Paragraph 3.1 here.

_____

2. Underline the controlling idea(s) in that topic sentence.

3. How is the controlling idea connected to the information in the paragraph?

_____

_____

ACTIVITY 7 | Writing topic sentences in paragraphs

Read the paragraphs and write a topic sentence for each. Be sure to indent the first line.

> **WORDS TO KNOW** Paragraphs 3.2 to 3.4
>
> **connection:** (n) an association
> **control:** (v) to manage
> **culture:** (n) the beliefs and actions of a group
> **depend (on):** (v) to need
>
> **effective:** (adj) useful
> **imagine:** (v) to make a picture in your head
> **in sum:** (connector) in conclusion

PARAGRAPH 3.2

Reasons for Playing Instruments

_____

_____

Some people learn to play a musical instrument because they want to have fun. They want to play it with their friends or maybe in a band. Other people learn to play an instrument because it is part of their **culture**. Certain instruments are popular in some cultures, such as the guitar in Spain or the oud[1] in the Middle East. Sometimes, people even learn to play an instrument because they think it will make them smarter. They want to keep their mind busy, and music is different from the work they think about all day long. **In sum,** there is clearly not just one main reason that people play a musical instrument.

[1]oud: a stringed instrument that is popular in the Middle East

PARAGRAPH 3.3

Differences between Modern Reptiles and Dinosaurs

_____

_____

One is size. Most modern reptiles are small. Dinosaurs were much larger than any reptile on Earth now. Second, the legs of most reptiles today are on the sides of their body. However, dinosaurs' legs were on the bottom of their body. In this way, dinosaurs could stand up on their back legs. Third, today's reptiles use the environment to **control** their body temperature. In contrast, dinosaurs controlled their own body temperature. They did not **depend on** what was around them. While reptiles and dinosaurs may seem very similar, they are actually very different.

A saltwater crocodile, the world's largest reptile

A hatchet

A Method for Learning New Words

_____

_____

_____

In the Keyword Method, language learners make a **connection** between the sound of the word they are trying to learn and a word in their first language. For example, a Japanese learner of English might connect the English word *hatchet* with the Japanese word *hachi*, which means "eight," because the two words have a similar sound. In the second step, learners make a picture in their heads to help them remember the word. In this case, the learner might **imagine** a person using a hatchet to cut down eight trees. For many language learners, the Keyword Method is **effective**.

Grammar: Complex Sentences

Three kinds of sentences are important for your writing: *simple, compound,* and *complex.*

* a **simple sentence** has one independent clause. An **independent clause** has one subject-verb relationship, and it can stand alone as a sentence.

   People from many different cultures **live** in Los Angeles.

* a **compound sentence** has two independent clauses that can stand alone. The two clauses are connected with words such as *and, but, so.*

   The weather there **is** hot, <u>and</u> **it** often **rains.**

* a **complex sentence** has one independent clause and one dependent clause Each clause has a subject-verb relationship. A **dependent clause** cannot stand alone. Here are two common types of dependent clauses.

TYPE OF DEPENDENT CLAUSE	EXAMPLES OF COMPLEX SENTENCES
An **adjective clause** gives more information about a noun it follows. It begins with a <u>relative pronoun</u> (*who/whom, that,* or *which*).	People <u>**who** exercise regularly</u> are healthier. Dictionaries <u>**that**</u> **have two languages** are useful.
An **adverb clause** begins with a <u>connecting word</u>, such as *because* (reason); *before, after, when* (time); *if* (condition); *although* (contrast).	They play the guitar <u>**because** they enjoy it.</u> <u>**Before** they start working</u>, they check email.

ACTIVITY 8 | Identifying types of sentences

Identify each sentence. Write *simple, compound,* or *complex.* Be ready to explain your answers.

1. _____ When I walked into the room, I was very nervous.

2. _____ Beijing has many famous tourist attractions, such as the Imperial Palace, Tian'anmen Square, and the Lama Temple.

3. _____ Central Park has a zoo and many other interesting places to visit, but sometimes it is too cold to visit in the winter.

4. _____ A good writer learns to create longer, more detailed sentences from simple ideas.

5. _____ Some families do not have the extra time that pets require.

6. _____ Although Bolívar's name is not as well-known outside Latin America, many people there consider him the most important historical person.

7. _____ Brazil and Chile are near each other, but these two South American countries are very different in geography, population, and language.

8. _____ Like most countries in South America, the majority of people in Chile speak Spanish.

9. _____ Before e-readers were invented, students had to carry several heavy books with them each day.

10. _____ E-readers are wireless, so students can carry them anywhere.

ACTIVITY 9 | Identifying types of complex sentences

Underline the dependent clause in each sentence. Write *Adj* if it is an adjective clause or *Adv* if it is an adverb clause.

1. _____ People who live in glass houses should not throw stones.

2. _____ If your photocopies cost 21 cents, your change should be four cents.

3. _____ Gumbo is a thick soup that is made with shrimp and vegetables.

4. _____ Bush became president after Clinton was president for eight years.

5. _____ The season that many young children enjoy a lot is summer.

6. _____ Because they do not go to school in summer, children often like summer more than other seasons.

7. _____ Most people become angry when their computer freezes.

8. _____ In class, we discussed problems that were common in the 1990s.

Mechanics: Commas

Commas are very important in writing because they help the reader understand the writer's message more easily.

EXPLANATION	EXAMPLES
Lists: A comma shows that a list has three or more things. We do not use a comma with two things. We use *and* instead of a comma.	I speak English, Spanish, and Japanese. I speak English and Spanish.
Compound sentences: A comma separates two independent clauses when there is a coordinating conjunction, such as *and, but, so, or.*	I speak three languages, **but** Adam speaks five.
Introductory words or phrases: A comma separates the subject from: • prepositional phrases (*In the winter of 1995, . . .*) • sequence words (*first, next, finally*) • transition words or phrases (*However, Therefore, In addition*)	**Last summer**, the beach lost a lot of sand. **First**, you will need to get a pencil. **Therefore**, we will not complete the project.
Adverb clauses: When the adverb clause is at the beginning of a sentence, use a comma after it. Do not use a comma if the adverb clause is at the end of a sentence.	**Because I speak three languages**, I can communicate with many people. I can communicate with many people **because I speak three languages**.

Note: For more information on commas, see Capitalization and Punctuation" in the *Writers Handbook.*

ACTIVITY 10 | Comma practice in sentences

Insert commas where necessary. Write the number of the comma rule/(s) (1, 2, 3, 4) on the line. Sometimes more than one rule is possible.

1. __2__ Brazil is surrounded by Spanish-speaking countries, but most people in Brazil speak Portuguese.

2. _____ The flags of Chile France and Norway have blue white and red sections.

3. _____ Fortunately no one was hurt in the accident that happened yesterday.

4. _____ Italian French Spanish and Portuguese came from Latin.

5. _____ My friend has an e-reader and she convinced me to buy one.

6. _____ In the summer of 1940 German soldiers entered France.

7. _____ Because English came from German there are many similar words in the two languages.

8. _____ If you want to make cookies you need flour sugar oil and vanilla.

ACTIVITY 11 | Comma practice in a paragraph

Insert six commas in the paragraph where necessary. Be prepared to explain your choices. Some sentences are correct with no commas.

> **WORDS TO KNOW** Paragraph 3.5
>
> **economy:** (n) the production of a place   **therefore:** (connector) as a result

Malaysia and Thailand

Because Malaysia and Thailand are next to each other we might think that these two countries share many similarities. In some ways, this is true. For example both countries are warm all year long. Both have many miles of beautiful beaches that attract tourists. In addition the **economy** of both countries is growing. However there are also several clear differences. For one, Malaysians and Thais speak completely different languages. The population of Malaysia is about 31 million while the population of Thailand is about 69 million. Thailand has a king, but Malaysia does not. Finally, Malaysia was part of Britain at one time but Thailand was never British. **Therefore** the fact that two countries are near each other does not always mean that they are similar.

Food vendor selling home-cooked local dishes at a street market stall, Sabah, Malaysia

BUILDING BETTER VOCABULARY

WORDS TO KNOW

addictive (adj)
advantage (n)
climb (v)
confuse (v)
connection (n)
contribution (n) AW
control (v)

culture (n) AW
depend (on) (v)
economy (n) AW
educational (adj)
effective (adj)
imagine (v)
immigrant (n) AW

improve (v)
in good shape (idiom)
in sum (connector) AW
investigator (n) AW
recognize (v)
reduce (v)
therefore (connector)

ACTIVITY 12 | Word associations

Circle the word or phrase that is more closely related to the bold word on the left.

1. climb	go down	go up
2. confuse	get it right	make a mistake
3. depend	need	try
4. economy	food	money
5. effective	useful	useless
6. imagine	speak	think
7. improve	better	worse
8. in sum	long	short
9. recognize	know	not know
10. therefore	but	so

ACTIVITY 13 | Collocations

Fill in the blank with the word that most naturally completes the phrase.

climb	contribution	effective	reduce	sum

1. _____ waste

2. a _____ to science

3. _____ a tree

4. a very _____ leader

5. in _____

advantage	connection	culture	depend	imagine

6. to have an _____

7. a _____ between two things

8. _____ on your parents for a place to live

9. _____ being in a car with no driver

10. normal in my _____

ACTIVITY 14 | Word forms

Complete each sentence with the correct word form. Use the correct forms of the words.

NOUN	VERB	ADJECTIVE	ADVERB	SENTENCES
connection	connect	connected		**1.** A conjunction such as *and* _____ two clauses.
				2. After you have _____ the wire to the TV, it should work.
				3. Argentina and Mexico share a historical _____.
culture		cultural	culturally	**4.** Argentina and Mexico may share a language, but they differ _____
				5. Many different _____ exist around the globe.
dependence	depend	dependent		**6.** Success in school _____ on many people.
effect		effective	effectively	**7.** One _____ of the new law is that teachers' salaries will not increase.
				8. What are _____ strategies for learning new vocabulary?
imagination	imagine	imaginary		**9.** In winter, I _____ I am in a warmer place.
				10. Experienced teachers encourage students to use their _____.

ACTIVITY 15 | Vocabulary in writing

Choose five words from Words to Know. Write a complete sentence with each word. Use *because, if, before, after, when, while,* or *although* in two of your sentences. Remember to use commas correctly.

1. _____

_____

2. _____

_____

3. _____

_____

4. _____

_____

5. _____

_____

BUILDING BETTER SENTENCES

ACTIVITY 16 | Editing

Each sentence has (x) number of errors. Find and correct them.

1. Although some politicians in this country believes that the new law will make a difference in electricity costs most people think there will be no change. (2)

2. In the sum, gasoline prices will continue to rise each year, because companies want make more money on gasoline sales. (3)

3. Although some teachers retire when they are 55 year old the normal retirement age for a teacher in U.K. is 60. (3)

4. Brazil ranks fifth in population and it is the fifth most big country in the world. (2)

5. According to the article people thought their dinner tasted better, when they did not use social media. (2)

6. When a airplane take off the pilot and other crew are very busy. (3)

ACTIVITY 17 | Writing sentences

Write an original sentence using the words listed. You may change the form of the nouns (singular/plural) and verbs (tenses).

1. (politician / years) *One of the local politicians has been in office for 18 years.*

2. (a new car / because) _____

3. (if / cancel) _____

4. (famous / France) _____

5. (average / price) _____

6. (one / most difficult) _____

ACTIVITY 18 | Combining sentences

Combine the ideas into one sentence. You may change the word forms, but do not change or omit any ideas. There may be more than one answer.

1. A condition requires attention.
   The condition is a medical condition.
   The condition is serious.
   The attention is immediate.

   _____

   _____

2. Canada is a country.
   Canada is large.
   The population of Canada is very small.

   _____

   _____

3. The assignment is to write a paper.
The assignment is the last one.
The assignment is for our history class.
The class is British History.
The paper should explain how the War of 1812 started.

_____

_____

WRITING

ACTIVITY 19 | Brainstorming ideas for a paragraph

Choose one of these topics. Brainstorm ideas about it and write your ideas in a list or on a diagram. When you have finished, circle the ideas that you think are best to include in a paragraph.

- animal communication
- international flights
- learning a language
- smartphones

ACTIVITY 20 | Writing a paragraph

Use your brainstorming notes from Activity 19 to write a paragraph. Follow these guidelines.

1. Begin your paragraph with a topic sentence that has a clear controlling idea.

2. Use at least two of the vocabulary words or phrases presented in Words to Know.

3. Make sure that your paragraph has the four features as outlined in Unit 1.

Elephants touching, to greet each other, Addo Elephant National Park, South Africa

ACTIVITY 21 | Peer editing

Work with a partner. Read your partner's paragraph from Activity 20. Use Peer Editing Form 3 in the *Writer's Handbook*. Offer positive suggestions to help your partner write a better paragraph. Consider your partner's comments as you revise your paragraph.

Additional Topics for Writing

Here are more ideas for writing a paragraph. When you write your paragraph, follow the guidelines for Activity 20.

TOPIC 1:   Look at the photo at the beginning of the unit. Write about a childhood memory of playing outside. Who were you with? How did you feel?

TOPIC 2:   Write about your daily routine. What do you do, and when? How many things do you do in a day? What is the best part of your day or week?

TOPIC 3:   Write about a famous person you would like to meet. What has this person done that is interesting to you? What would you talk about? What would you hope to learn from the experience?

TOPIC 4:   Write about two vacation destinations. Which is better? Compare the sights. What is similar, and what is different? What are some activities you can do while in each of these places?

TOPIC 5:   Write about your favorite relative. Who is this person? What qualities make this person special? How does this person make others feel?

TEST PREP

You should spend about 25 minutes on this task. Write about the following topic:

In your opinion, why do so many people want to learn English?

Give reasons for your answer and include any relevant examples from your knowledge or experience. Remember to include a topic sentence with a controlling idea. Write at least 150 words.

TIP

Be sure that your topic sentence has a logical controlling idea. Remember that your topic sentence guides your paragraph. If the topic sentence is not clear, the reader will have difficulty following your supporting ideas.

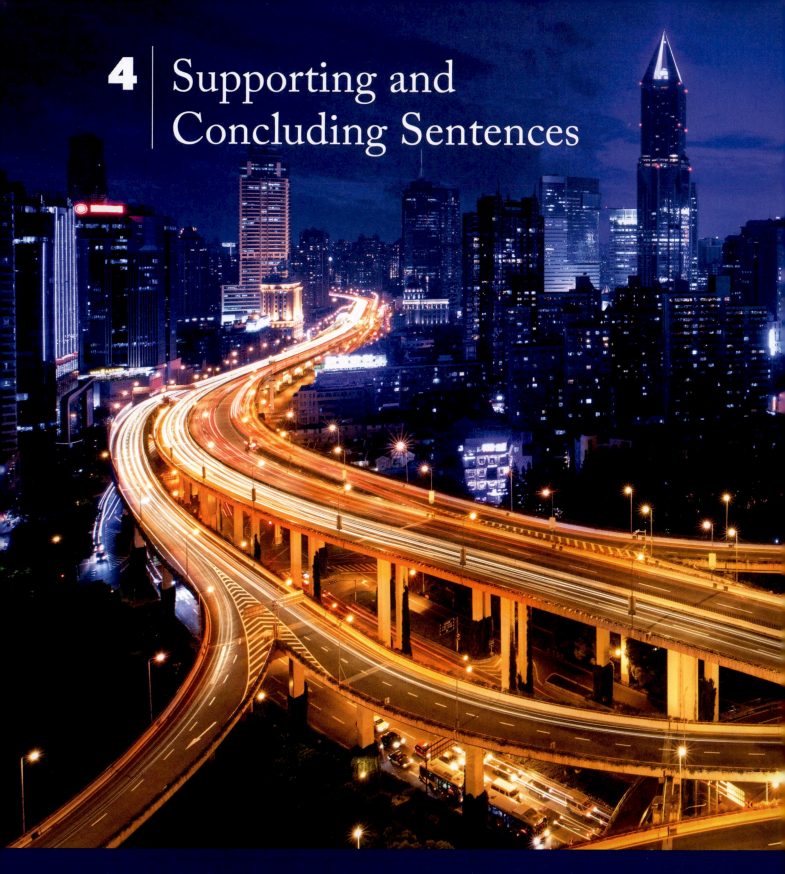

4 | Supporting and Concluding Sentences

Elevated highways at night,
Shanghai China

FREEWRITE | Look at the photo and write any ideas you have about the city, the roads and where they lead, and the feeling of driving on them at night. Write five to ten sentences.

ELEMENTS OF GREAT WRITING

What Are Supporting Sentences?

Supporting sentences give information that explains and expands on the topic sentence. They provide the details of the paragraph. They answer questions such as *Who? What? Where? When? Why?* and *How?* Good writers think about answers to questions like these when they write.

Remember that the controlling idea in the topic sentence guides the content of your supporting sentences.

ACTIVITY 1 | Predicting supporting content

Read each topic sentence. Circle the topic. Underline the controlling idea. Then predict the kind of supporting information you will find in the paragraph.

1. Although New York and Boston attract millions of tourists, one of the best cities to visit in the eastern United States is Washington, D.C.

   What kind of supporting information do you expect in this paragraph?

   _____

   _____

   _____

2. The Grand Palace is one of the most popular tourist destinations in Thailand.

   What kind of supporting information do you expect in this paragraph?

   _____

   _____

   _____

3. One of the people I admire the most is my great-grandmother Carla.

   What kind of supporting information do you expect in this paragraph?

   _____

   _____

   _____

ACTIVITY 2 | Checking your predictions

Read the three paragraphs. The supporting sentences are highlighted in blue. Look at your predictions in Activity 1. How well did you predict the supporting information? Discuss your predictions and results with a partner.

> **WORDS TO KNOW** Paragraphs 4.1 to 4.3
>
> **amazed:** (adj) surprised
> **complain:** (v) to express unhappiness with a thing or person or situation
> **construction:** (n) the act of building
> **destination:** (n) a place someone travels to
>
> **opportunity:** (n) a chance to do something
> **style:** (n) a way of doing something
> **surround:** (v) to be on all sides
> **survive:** (v) to continue to live or exist after a difficult or dangerous situation

PARAGRAPH 4.1

A Great Tourist Destination

Although New York and Boston attract millions of tourists, one of the best cities to visit in the eastern United States is Washington, D.C. First, Washington has some of the most interesting landmarks[1] in the country. There are several beautiful memorials[2] to early U.S. presidents, including the Lincoln Memorial, the Jefferson Memorial, and the Washington Monument. There is also a tour of the White House, which is the home of the president of the United States. Second, Washington has wonderful museums that are free to visit. The Smithsonian Institution is a large group of museums that offers excellent **opportunities** to learn about everything from natural history to aerospace. Finally, Georgetown is a historic area in the northwest part of Washington that has shopping, restaurants, and entertainment for the whole family. Washington, D.C., does not have the large number of visitors that New York or Boston has, but this important city is one of the best **destinations** for tourists.

[1]landmark: a historic building; a well-known location
[2]memorial: a statue or some other structure that helps people remember something or someone

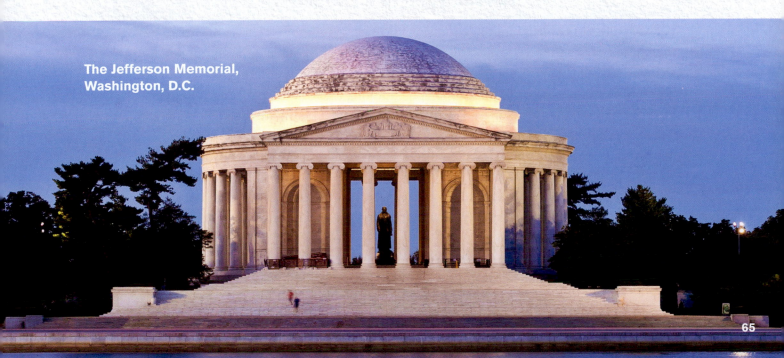

The Jefferson Memorial, Washington, D.C.

PARAGRAPH 4.2

The Grand Palace in Bangkok

The Grand Palace is one of the most popular tourist destinations in Thailand. The **construction** of the palace began in 1782, and the kings and royal families lived there until 1925. The palace area is more than 2 million square feet (185,806 square meters), and the wall that **surrounds** the palace is more than 6,000 feet (1829 meters) long. This large area includes several buildings, gardens, and special rooms with a mix of Asian and European **styles**. It is a beautiful place with a lot of history, so it is easy to understand why so many tourists visit the Grand Palace each year.

PARAGRAPH 4.3

An Immigrant in the Family

One of the people I admire the most is my great-grandmother Carla. She came to the United States from Italy in 1911 as a young woman. Like many other immigrants at that time, she had nothing when she arrived. Soon after her arrival **in** New York, she began working as a seamstress[1] in Brooklyn. Not long after that, she met and married my great-grandfather. They immediately began their large family. Great-grandma Carla had eight children—five boys and three girls. In addition to taking care of such a large family in a new country, my great-grandmother **survived** discrimination[2] as a foreigner, two World Wars, the Great Depression[3], and a long list of illnesses. However, she almost never **complained**, and she was very happy with her new life in America. If you learn more about my great-grandmother Carla, you, too, will be **amazed** at her life.

[1]seamstress: a woman who makes clothing
[2]discrimination: unfair treatment
[3]the Great Depression: a period of difficult economic times in the U.S. between 1929 and 1939

What do Supporting Sentences Do?

Supporting sentences have different goals. Writers use them to do one or more of the following:

- **Explain:** When she was 10 years old, her family left their farm for economic reasons.
- **Describe:** They lived in a beautiful three-story castle in the middle of the forest.
- **Give reasons:** Some people quit their jobs because of the difficult working conditions.
- **Give facts:** More than 10 percent of this university's student population is international.
- **Give examples:** For example, California is the top producer of peaches, grapes, and strawberries.
- **Define:** Gumbo is a thick soup made of seafood and meat served over rice.

ACTIVITY 3 | Identifying supporting sentences

Look back at Paragraphs 4.1–4.3. What are the goals of the supporting sentences? Compare your answers with a partner. More than one goal is possible. Be prepared to explain your answers.

1. What are the goals of the supporting sentences in Paragraph 4.1? _____

   _____

2. What are the goals of the supporting sentences in Paragraph 4.2? _____

   _____

3. What are the goals of the supporting sentences in Paragraph 4.3? _____

   _____

ACTIVITY 4 | Writing topic sentences

For each topic, brainstorm some ideas on a separate piece of paper. Then write a topic sentence with a controlling idea. Circle the controlling ideas.

1. vacation: _Orlando, Florida, is the best vacation destination for children_

2. mathematics: _____

   _____

3. a family member _____

   _____

4. an animal or pet _____

   _____

5. a best friend: _____

_____

6. a restaurant: _____

_____

ACTIVITY 5 | Asking for more information

Choose three of your topic sentences from Activity 4 and write them below. Then write three questions about each topic. Use *wh-* questions.

1. Topic Sentence: ___Orlando, Florida, is the best vacation destination for children.___

a. ___Why do children like Orlando?___

b. _____

c. _____

2. Topic Sentence: _____

_____

a. _____

b. _____

c. _____

3. Topic Sentence: _____

_____

a. _____

b. _____

c. _____

WRITER'S NOTE Staying on Track

As you write a paragraph. you should always look back at your topic sentence. Do not include any information that is unrelated to the topic sentence. It is very easy to lose track of the main idea if you do not refer to the topic sentence from time to time. By asking questions about your topic sentence after you are finished writing, you can better identify the content that should stay in your paragraph and the content that you should remove from your paragraph.

Avoiding Unrelated Information

Sometimes writers give information that is not closely related to the topic. When this happens, the paragraph does not read smoothly, and the reader might get confused about the writer's message. Each sentence in a paragraph should be connected to the controlling idea or ideas in the topic sentence of the paragraph.

ACTIVITY 6 | Identifying the unrelated sentence

Read Paragraphs 4.4–4.6. In each paragraph, cross out the sentence that is unrelated to the controlling idea(s) in the topic sentence.

WORDS TO KNOW Paragraphs 4.4 to 4.6

continent: (n) one of the main large land areas on the earth
disagree: (v) to not agree
option: (n) a choice
perfectly: (adv) without any errors or problems

research: (v) to study carefully
tremendously: (adv) a great deal; very much
unless: (conj) if not
used to: (aux v) means "was done in the past, but is not true now"

PARAGRAPH 4.4

Dining at Fresh Market

The menu at Fresh Market in downtown Springfield has five main dishes, which are simple but very delicious. My number one dish there is pasta with fresh vegetables. The pasta is cooked **perfectly**, and the vegetables include broccoli, onions, tomatoes, and corn. My second favorite main dish is the spicy chicken and brown rice soup. The chicken is a little hot for some people's tastes, but many people really like the fact that you get brown rice instead of the more boring white rice. The other main dishes are fried chicken with curry potatoes, Greek salad with grilled shrimp, and fried fish with vinegar chips. All three of these use the freshest ingredients and taste great. The food at Paul's Bistro is also very good. If you eat a meal at Fresh Market, I am sure you will enjoy it **tremendously**.

NORTH AMERICA

EUROPE

ASIA

AFRICA

SOUTH AMERICA

AUSTRALIA

ANTARCTICA

PARAGRAPH 4.5

Counting the Continents

It seems like the number of **continents** would be a simple fact, but actually, the number depends on where you live. In the United States, for example, students learn that there are seven continents. These seven are North America, South America, Europe, Africa, Asia, Australia, and Antarctica. In Europe, however, many students learn that there are six continents. They learn that North America and South America are one continent, which they call *the Americas*. Panama is the southern end of North America, but it **used to** be part of Colombia, which is in South America. In some countries, Europe and Asia are combined into one continent called Eurasia. In others, Antarctica is not considered a continent. It is interesting that different regions **disagree** on the definition of *continent*. Perhaps in the future, all countries will agree on what a continent is and how many there are on Earth.

PARAGRAPH 4.6

Traveling between Rome and Paris

There are three good **options** for traveling between Rome and Paris. The fastest way is by plane. However, flying between these two cities can be a little expensive **unless** you can find a cheap airline ticket. The second way is by train, which is very popular with many tourists. In fact, Rome and Paris are visited each year by millions of students from all over. The train is not expensive and the service is very good, but the overnight trip takes about 14 hours. Finally, many people take a bus. The bus is the cheapest of the three options, but it takes up to 22 hours, which means it takes the most time. If tourists **research** each of these three travel options, they will certainly find an option that works well for them.

ACTIVITY 7 | Explaining supporting and unrelated sentences

Read the paragraph. For each of the underlined, numbered supporting sentences, choose *related* or *unrelated*. Then write a reason for your answer.

WORDS TO KNOW Paragraph 4.7

laundry: (n) dirty clothing to wash
protective: (adj) concerned for safety

strict: (adj) requiring obedience

PARAGRAPH 4.7

Strict Parents

Fortunately, my parents were very **strict** with me when I was a child. I think that they were **protective** because I was an only child. However, at that time, it felt like I was in prison. I had to come home after school and immediately do my homework. ¹After I finished my homework, I was allowed to watch only one hour of television. While my friends were playing video games or watching cartoons, I was usually doing things around the house to help my mother. ²This included doing some of the **laundry**, taking care of the yard, and helping to prepare dinner. ³My father was an architect, and my mother was a housewife. Looking back, I am not sorry that my parents were strict with me because I think it was the best way for a child to grow up.

---

1. related / unrelated   Reason: _____

_____

2. related / unrelated   Reason: _____

_____

3. related / unrelated   Reason: _____

_____

Using Pronouns in Place of Key Nouns

Because a paragraph is about one topic, writers often repeat key nouns from the topic sentence in their supporting sentences. However, too much repetition of these same nouns can sound awkward. You can avoid repeating key nouns by using pronouns. Be sure to use the correct singular or plural pronoun.

EXPLANATION	EXAMPLES
Pronouns take the place of a person, place, or thing. Carla ➝ She Washington ➝ It Giraffes ➝ They	One of the best cities to visit on the East Coast of the United States is **Washington, DC. It** has some of the most interesting tourist spots in the country. One of the people I most admire is **my great-grandmother. She** came to the United States from Italy in 1911.
Remember to be consistent. If you use *they* at the beginning of a paragraph, do not switch to *it*.	✓ **Giraffes** are among the most interesting of all the animals that live in Africa. **They** are easily recognized by **their** special features. ✗ They have long necks and long legs, but <u>its</u> neck is longer than <u>its</u> legs.

ACTIVITY 8 | Identifying key nouns and pronouns

Write the correct pronoun. Use *it*, *they*, or *we*. Then underline the key noun that the pronoun refers to.

1. <u>Tennis rackets</u> have changed tremendously in the last 10 years. _They_ used to be small and heavy, but that is no longer true.

2. Soccer is by far the most widely played sport in the world. _____ is played professionally on nearly every continent.

3. I will never forget my childhood friends Carlos and Juan and what _____ taught me.

4. Not only is text messaging fast, but _____ is also an interesting way to practice English.

5. A bad thing happened to my classmates and me at school yesterday. _____ were late coming to class and missed a quiz.

6. If you travel to Budapest, Hungary, you will fall in love with the Danube River. _____ separates the city into two parts—Buda and Pest.

7. Here is a photo of me and my family last year. _____ were on vacation in Paris.

8. The Grand Canyon is over a mile (6,093 feet/1,857 meters) deep. _____ was formed over millions of years by the Colorado River and other smaller rivers.

Grammar: Avoiding Fragments

EXPLANATION	EXAMPLES
A **sentence fragment** is not a complete sentence. Often it is: • without a subject, a verb, or both • a dependent clause, which is never a complete sentence To correct a sentence fragment: • add a subject or verb • combine two clauses with a connector	✗ I went to Italy last summer. <u>Was a wonderful trip.</u> ✗ Students do not often major in art. <u>Because they worry about job opportunities.</u> ✓ I went to Italy last summer. **It** was a wonderful trip. ✓ Students do not often major in art **because** they worry about job opportunities.

ACTIVITY 9 | Correcting sentence fragments

Work with a partner. Discuss what the problem is in each sentence. Then write a correct sentence. More than one correction may be possible.

1. One of the most common reasons that people decide to become a vegetarian.

   One of the most common reasons that people decide to become a vegetarian is to improve their health.

2. Because the wind and rain were so strong when the airplane tried to take off.

   _____

   _____

3. Although the price of gasoline is extremely high at the current time.

   _____

   _____

4. In order to fly to an international destination.

   _____

   _____

5. For some teachers, a fragment a very serious type of mistake because shows a lack of understanding of the structure of a sentence.

   _____

   _____

Grammar: Avoiding Run-Ons and Comma Splices

EXPLANATION	EXAMPLES
A **run-on sentence** combines two independent clauses (complete sentences) without punctuation or a conjunction. To correct a run-on sentence: • separate the sentences into two with a period • add a connector	✗ I went to <u>Italy I</u> did not visit Milan. ✓ I went to Italy. I did not visit Milan. ✓ I went to Italy, **but** I did not visit Milan. ✓ **Though** I went to Italy, I did not visit Milan.
A **comma splice** occurs when two independent clauses are separated by a comma. To correct a comma splice: • add a connecting word after the comma • create two sentences from the one	✗ I went to Italy last <u>summer, it</u> was a great trip. ✓ I went to Italy last summer, **and** it was a great trip. ✓ I went to Italy last summer. **It** was a great trip.

ACTIVITY 10 | Correcting run-on sentences and comma splices

Discuss the type of error in each sentence with a partner. Write *RO* for run-on sentence or *CS* for comma splice. Then write a correct sentence. More than one correction may be possible.

1. __CS__ A whale is one of the largest animals on Earth, few people have seen one.

   A whale is one of the largest animals on Earth. Few people have seen one.

   OR Although the whale is one of the largest animals on Earth, few people have seen one.

   _____

2. _____ Language-learning software helps students learn languages, many students buy this software in addition to their class books.

   _____

   _____

3. _____ It is a difficult time for many people, however, people are strong and they will survive.

   _____

   _____

4. _____ *Dancing with the Stars* is a well-known television show the dancing is very exciting.

   _____

   _____

5. _____ This magazine has great articles on international events it won awards last year.

   _____

   _____

What Is a Concluding Sentence?

The **concluding sentence** is the last sentence of a paragraph. It concludes, or ends, a paragraph. It tells the reader that you have finished talking about the idea introduced by the topic sentence.

A concluding sentence often has one or more of these four purposes:

- **It restates the main idea.** It summarizes the main idea or points in the paragraph. Often it says about the same thing as the topic sentence, but in different words.
- **It offers a suggestion.** It tells readers something they should think or do.
- **It gives an opinion.** It tells readers the writer's thoughts or beliefs about the topic.
- **It makes a prediction.** It tells readers what might happen in the future.

The following are transitional words and phrases commonly used at the beginning of a concluding sentence. There is usually a comma after the transitional word or phrase.

As a result,	Clearly,	Therefore,	Surely,
Certainly,	Overall,	Thus,	For these reasons,
In conclusion,	Because of this,	For this reason,	In brief,

ACTIVITY 11 | Analyzing concluding sentences

Look back and read the topic sentence and the concluding sentence from each paragraph listed below. Write the concluding sentence. Then discuss with a partner which purpose listed above best fits each concluding sentence.

1. Paragraph 4.1 "A Great Tourist Destination"

   Concluding Sentence: _____

   _____

2. Paragraph 4.3 "An Immigrant in the Family"

   Concluding Sentence: _____

   _____

3. Paragraph 4.4 "My Dining Experience at Fresh Market"

   Concluding Sentence: _____

   _____

4. Paragraph 4.6 "Traveling between Rome and Paris"

   Concluding Sentence: _____

   _____

ACTIVITY 12 | Analyzing paragraphs

Read the paragraphs and complete these tasks for each one.

1. Underline the topic sentence.
2. Cross out the sentence that is not an appropriate supporting sentence.
3. Write a concluding sentence on the lines provided.

> **WORDS TO KNOW** Paragraphs 4.8 to 4.10
>
> **amount:** (n) how much (of something)
> **assign:** (v) to give tasks to do
> **due to:** (prep) because of
>
> **replace:** (v) to change one thing for another
> **shallow:** (adj) not deep

PARAGRAPH 4.8

Adjusting to College Life

When I started college, I was surprised at the **amount** of studying that was necessary. I had to change my study habits. In high school, I rarely studied, yet my grades were good. In college, all my professors thought their class was the most important. My favorite class in college was British History. Each professor **assigned** a tremendous amount of homework. As a result, my free time became very limited. Reading assignments, group projects, and research **replaced** my time with friends. My classes kept me so busy that I only saw my friends on Saturday nights. This schedule was a big change from high school, where I used to play sports, have fun, and see my friends several times a week. _____

_____

PARAGRAPH 4.9

Four Ways to Cook an Egg

There are at least four easy ways to cook an egg. The first and probably the easiest way is to boil it. It is the easiest way because the egg is not opened. Just drop the egg into a pot of water and boil it for eight minutes. Another easy way is to scramble it. All you need is a fork to mix the egg before you put it into a hot frying pan. A third way is to fry it "over easy." Just put the egg into the pan without breaking the yellow center (the yolk). After a minute or so, turn the egg over to cook it on the other side. Finally, poaching involves cooking the egg in boiling water. Break the egg into a small metal cup that is sitting in a pan of very hot, **shallow** water. Poaching an egg takes only five minutes. Some people believe that brown eggs taste better than white eggs. _____

_____

Different Names for the Same Kind of Storm

When bad weather, thunder, and strong winds mix, the result is a dangerous storm, but the name for that storm differs according to where the storm occurs. When a big storm forms in the Atlantic or eastern Pacific Ocean, it is called a "hurricane." This type of storm can be dangerous to people living in the United States, Mexico, Central America, or the Caribbean Islands. When a large storm begins in the southern Pacific Ocean, this same type of storm is called a "cyclone." Cyclones are less common than hurricanes **due to** the colder temperature of the water in the southern Pacific Ocean. Finally, if this same storm begins in the northwestern Pacific Ocean, it is referred to as a "typhoon." Typhoons hit areas such as Japan, Guam, or the Philippines.

A satellite photo of Hurricane Isabel nearing the North Carolina, USA, coast on September 17, 2003

BUILDING BETTER VOCABULARY

WORDS TO KNOW

amazed (adj)	due to (prep)	shallow (adj) AW
amount (n)	laundry (n)	strict (adj)
assign (v) AW	opportunity (n)	style (n) AW
complain (v)	option (n) AW	surround (v)
construction (n) AW	perfectly (adv)	survive (v) AW
continent (n) AW	protective (adj)	tremendously (adv)
destination (n) AW	replace (v)	unless (conj)
disagree (v)	research (v) AW	used to (aux v)

ACTIVITY 13 | Word associations

Circle the word or phrase that is more closely related to the bold word on the left.

1. construction	building	meeting
2. continents	Austria and England	Asia and Europe
3. destination	travel	worry
4. due to	error	reason
5. laundry	clothing	money
6. opportunities	chances	changes
7. options	choices	occupations
8. shallow	not strong	not deep
9. surround	for a long time	on all sides
10. survive	continue buying	continue living

ACTIVITY 14 | Collocations

Fill in the blank with the word that most naturally completes the phrase.

amazed	complain	disagree	replace	survive

1. _____ a broken phone

2. _____ about a slow computer

3. _____ an automobile accident

4. _____ on a solution

5. _____ by a performance

due to	perfectly	style	tremendously	unless

6. _____ the problem is solved

7. _____ the bad weather

8. a different _____ of

9. to enjoy something _____

10. do something _____

ACTIVITY 15 | Word forms

Complete each sentence with the correct word form. Use the correct forms of the words.

NOUN	VERB	ADJECTIVE	ADVERB	SENTENCES
assignment	assign			**1.** Our teacher _____ our group the most difficult topic. **2.** The _____ was fun.
construction	construct			**3.** It is difficult to _____ certain kinds of houses in very cold climates. **4.** The _____ of that kind of office building is very expensive.
perfection	perfect	perfect	perfectly	**5.** You do not need to speak English _____ to go to a university. **6.** For many people, eating dessert is the _____ way to end a good meal.
replacement	replace			**7.** To fix the engine, the driver had to wait for the delivery of a _____ part. **8.** To spell the plural of nouns ending in -*y*, _____ *y* with *i*, and add -*es*.
		tremendous	tremendously	**9.** When the plane crashed, there was a _____ explosion. **10.** Most people say they enjoyed the movie _____ .

ACTIVITY 16 | Vocabulary in writing

Choose five words from Words to Know. Write a complete sentence with each word. Write one simple sentence, two compound sentences, and two complex sentences.

1. _____

_____

2. _____

_____

3. _____

_____

4. _____

_____

5. _____

_____

BUILDING BETTER SENTENCES

ACTIVITY 17 | Editing

Each sentence has (x) number of errors. Find and correct them.

1. People use cell phones for many purposes, it is very important in daily life. (3)

2. Wimbledon is the home of a major tennis competition international every summers. (2)

3. Some professors requires students to submit all drafts of an essay so is important to prepare each draft careful. (4)

4. An example of a even number is 24, an example of a odd number is 27. (4)

5. Although some people in the U.S. are like to drink the tea most people prefers coffee. (4)

ACTIVITY 18 | Putting a paragraph together

Look at the photo. Then discuss in a small group other ways people commonly use cell phones. Complete the three sentences so they fit in a paragraph that begins with the topic sentence given. Write your own concluding sentence.

Topic Sentence: People use cell phones for many things other than calling someone.

Supporting Sentence 1: According to many studies, the number one use of cell phones is for texting. People find texting more convenient than calling.

Supporting Sentence 2: Another common use

Supporting Sentence 3: An unusual, but growing use

Concluding Sentence:

ACTIVITY 19 | Combining sentences

Combine the ideas into one sentence. You may change the word forms, but do not change or omit any ideas. There may be more than one way to combine sentences.

1. People want to visit Paris.
   The people are from all over the world.
   There are reasons to do this.
   Their reasons are similar.
   Its food is great.
   Its architecture is beautiful.

   _____

   _____

2. Diets are preferred by many athletes.
   The diets are high-protein.
   The athletes are serious.

   _____

   _____

3. Each professor assigned homework.
   The homework was every night.
   The amount of homework was tremendous.
   This happened when I was a first-year university student.

   _____

   _____

WRITING

ACTIVITY 20 | Writing a paragraph

Choose one of the topic sentences from Activity 5. Write a paragraph about the topic. Follow these guidelines.

1. In your supporting sentences, answer the questions that you wrote in Activity 5. Remember to write only about ideas that are introduced in the controlling idea of your topic sentence.

2. Write a concluding sentence for your paragraph.

3. Use at least two of the words in Words to Know. Underline these words in your paragraph.

ACTIVITY 21 | Peer editing

Work with a partner. Read your partner's paragraph from Activity 20. Use Peer Editing Form 4 in the *Writer's Handbook*. Offer positive suggestions to help your partner write a better paragraph. Consider your partner's comments as you revise your paragraph.

Additional Topics for Writing

Here are more ideas for writing a paragraph. When you write your paragraph, follow the guidelines in Activity 20.

TOPIC 1: Look at the photo at the beginning of the unit. What are some reasons why traditional jobs or crafts become less common? Is this good, bad, or a little of both?

TOPIC 2: Write about a person that you know and admire. What special qualities does this person have? What does this person do?

TOPIC 3: Write about a great career for today's job market. What kind of job is it? What skills would someone need? What are the benefits of doing this kind of job?

TOPIC 4: Give some advice about doing something, such as buying a car or choosing a school. What should someone know? What steps should the person follow?

TOPIC 5: Write about your perfect travel destination. Where would it be? Why is this a good place for you to be? What would you do there?

TEST PREP

> **TIP**
>
> Underline key words in the writing prompt. Some examples of key words are *explain, describe, compare,* and *in your opinion.* Always look back at the key words as you write to be sure you are answering the question correctly and staying on topic.

You should spend about 25 minutes on this task. Write about the following topic:

In your opinion, is it a good idea to allow students to have cell phones at school?

Give three reasons to support your opinion. Include a concluding sentence. Remember to avoid sentence fragments, run-on sentences, and comma splices. Write at least 150 words.

5 | Paragraph Review

OBJECTIVES
- Review the features of a paragraph
- Review grammar, mechanics, and punctuation
- Use articles correctly in writing
- Write a paragraph

A mother grizzly bear and her cubs stop traffic on Denali's 92-mile-long Park Road in Denali National Park, Alaska, USA.

FREEWRITE | Look at the photo and use your imagination to complete a paragraph beginning: *One day, I was driving to . . . when I saw three bears walking down the road.* Write five to ten sentences.

ELEMENTS OF GREAT WRITING

Four Features of a Good Paragraph: Review

You have learned that:

1. the first line of a paragraph is indented
2. a **paragraph** has a **topic sentence** that states the **main idea**
3. all of the sentences in the paragraph relate to the main idea
4. the **concluding sentence** ends the paragraph logically

ACTIVITY 1 | Writing topic sentences

Read the paragraphs. Write a topic sentence for each one. Remember to state the topic and include a controlling idea. Indent the first line.

> **WORDS TO KNOW** Paragraphs 5.1 to 5.2
>
> **apply:** (v) to ask for
> **attempt:** (v) to try
> **former:** (adj) previous
>
> **narrow:** (adj) having a very small space; the opposite of wide
> **submit:** (v) to send

PARAGRAPH 5.1

Applying to a College or University

_____

_____

Applicants need to know that there is a college for every student. It might be a small private college, a large state school, a community college[1], or a public university. The final choice of a school depends on students' needs and wishes. When they are ready to **apply**, students should first make a list of schools that they are interested in. If their list is long, they should shorten it to five or six. The next step is to find out the requirements for each school. Applicants should be sure to organize the correct records and information. Most applications require students to **submit** letters of recommendation[2], so students should be thinking about who will write their letters. Students can ask a **former** teacher, sports coach, or other adult to write a letter. The third step is to fill out the application for each school on their list. If an essay is required, students should do their best to make sure the language in their essay is interesting, well organized, and correct. The final step is for students to visit the schools they hope to attend. Parents often take their children to see many colleges. If applicants follow these steps, they should have a better chance of gaining admission to a school that is right for their personality and career goals.

[1]community college: a two-year college
[2]letter of recommendation: a letter written for a person applying for something

The Amazing Capilano Bridge

It is 450 feet (137 meters) long. It is 230 feet (70 meters) above the Capilano River in British Columbia, Canada. The original wood and rope bridge was built in 1889 to help people cross the deep canyon[1]. However, today only tourists **attempt** to cross this **narrow** bridge. They simply want to enjoy the beautiful Canadian nature around the bridge. The view as you are walking across the bridge is breathtaking[2]. Without a doubt, the Capilano Bridge is an amazing place to visit.

[1]canyon: a very deep open space between two areas of land
[2]breathtaking: causing great surprise or wonder

The Capilano Bridge in Vancouver, Canada

ACTIVITY 2 | Writing supporting sentences

Read the paragraph. Then study the supporting sentences for the first and third ways to avoid a cold. Write a supporting sentence or two for the second way.

> **WORDS TO KNOW** Paragraphs 5.3
>
> **increase:** (v) to go up in number, amount   **spread:** (v) move from one person to another

PARAGRAPH 5.3

How to Avoid Being Sick with a Cold

There are three ways to avoid becoming sick with a cold. The first way is to wash your hands several times during the day. Washing with soap helps kill germs[1] that can **spread** a cold from someone else to you. The second way is to eat foods that have lots of vitamin C. _____

_____

_____

Finally, a very important step to avoid getting sick is to be well rested. This means you should sleep for at least six hours every night. Being tired makes your body weaker, and this **increases** the chance of getting sick. I suggest following these simple recommendations to avoid getting a cold.

[1]germs: small living things that can cause illnesses or disease

ACTIVITY 3 | Writing concluding sentences

Look back at Paragraphs 5.1 and 5.2. Write a different concluding sentence for each paragraph. Remember that a concluding sentence can restate the main idea, make a suggestion, give an opinion, or make a prediction. Share your sentences with a partner.

Paragraph 5.1 Concluding Sentence: _____

_____

Paragraph 5.2 Concluding Sentence: _____

_____

Mechanics: Review

You have learned

- to use capitalization, end punctuation, and commas correctly.
  See "Capitalization and Punctuation" in the Writer's Handbook for more information.

ACTIVITY 4 | Editing

Read the paragraphs. Each has seven errors in capitalization and punctuation (commas, periods, question marks). Find and correct the mistakes.

WORDS TO KNOW Paragraphs 5.4 to 5.5

guard: (v) to protect; to watch carefully
pour: (v) to move liquid or other contents from one container to another
score: (v) to earn points in a game

spill: (v) to cause or allow liquid to fall from a container
stir: (v) to mix the contents of a liquid

PARAGRAPH 5.4

How Hockey Is Played

There is a lot to know about the sport of hockey. Hockey is popular in many countries, including Canada and the United states, the game is played on ice and the players wear skates to move around. Hockey players can **score** a point if they hit a special disk called a *puck* into the goal. However, this is not as easy as it seems because a special player called a Goalie **guards** the goal. The goalie's job is to keep the puck away from the goal, the next time you see a hockey game on television, perhaps you will be able to follow the action better, because you have this information.

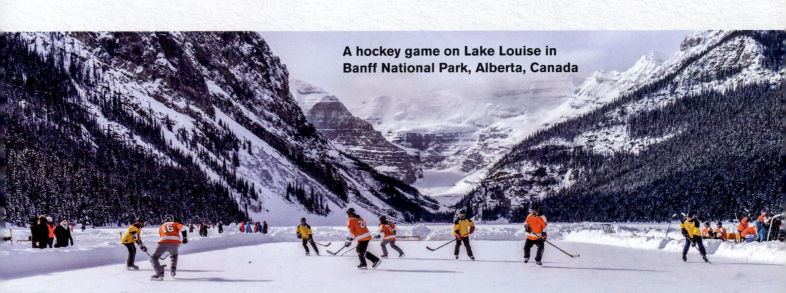

A hockey game on Lake Louise in Banff National Park, Alberta, Canada

A Unique Drink from Southeast Asia

Teh Tarik is a popular beverage[1] that is served in restaurants and markets in some asian countries, such as Malaysia, and Singapore. Teh Tarik is made with tea and milk, and its name means "pulled tea." To make Teh Tarik, add four tablespoons of black tea to boiling water Allow the mixture to cook on a low fire for five minutes. Then **pour** the tea into a separate cup, and add four tablespoons of condensed milk[2]. **Stir** the mixture briefly. With your hands far apart, pour the mixture into an empty cup in your other hand. Then pour the mixture back into the original cup. Do this several times. Be careful not to **spill** it. As you do this, it looks like you are pulling the tea and this explains the name of this delicious drink. when the mixture is thick and has a white top, pour it into a clear glass drinking this wonderful tea is as enjoyable as watching someone prepare it.

[1]beverage: any kind of drink
[2]condensed milk: a thick sweet milk product

A Teh Tarik shop in Singapore

Correct the 10 comma mistakes in the student paragraph. For information on commas, see Capitalization and Punctuation in the *Writer's Handbook*.

WORDS TO KNOW Paragraph 5.6

ought to: (aux v) should
site: (n) a place; a location

spot: (n) a place; a location

PARAGRAPH 5.6

A Great Place to Visit in California

If you go to California San Diego is a great **spot** to visit, because of the many exciting things to see and do there. First you should visit the Gaslamp Quarter. In this historic area, you can easily find great food fun and culture. Next, you should visit SeaWorld to see the amazing animal shows. After you visit SeaWorld you should see a football or baseball game at Qualcomm Stadium. Finally you **ought to** see the animals at the world-famous San Diego Zoo. If you decide to go to the zoo do not forget to see the giant pandas. If you visit one two or all three of these San Diego **sites**, you will certainly have a fun and interesting trip.

A panda at the San Diego Zoo

Maintaining Paragraph Unity

It is important to be able to identify the topic, topic sentence, and writer's purpose in a paragraph. It is also important to make sure that all the supporting sentences relate to the topic sentence. Remember to refer to the controlling idea in the topic sentence to see that each supporting sentence relates to it.

ACTIVITY 6 | Identifying unrelated supporting sentences

Read each paragraph. Cross out the unrelated supporting sentence.

> **WORDS TO KNOW** Paragraphs 5.7 to 5.8
>
> **adapt:** (v) to change
> **available:** (adj) easy to find
> **harsh:** (adj) difficult; severe
>
> **hide:** (v) to make oneself difficult to see
> **remarkable:** (adj) amazing; extraordinary

PARAGRAPH 5.7

Japan's Incredible Snow Monkeys

In Japan, snow monkeys are very interesting animals that have **adapted** in several ways to the cold winters. First, they travel less in the winter and spend more time in hot springs[1] to stay warm. Thousands of tourists come to see these interesting monkeys every spring. Many snow monkeys sleep in trees to avoid being covered by the heavy snow that can fall during the night. In addition, their very thick hair protects them from extremely cold temperatures. Snow monkeys also change their diet during the winter. During warmer months, they eat fruits, seeds, young leaves, and other foods. When these foods are not **available** in winter, snow monkeys find food in the ground or eat fish from the hot springs. These **remarkable** changes allow snow monkeys to live farther north than any other monkey in the world and make this animal one of the most interesting on Earth.

[1]spring: a small stream of water coming out of the Earth

**Snow monkeys (Japanese macaques)
bathing in hot springs in Nagano, Japan**

Bears of the Arctic

Polar bears have unique bodies that help them live in the **harsh** weather of the Arctic. They are large animals that weigh up to 1,800 pounds (817 kilograms). The body fat from all this weight helps keep them warm. Their heavy white fur not only protects them from icy winds but also helps them **hide** in the heavy snow. It snows a lot in the Arctic. The bears have five long sharp claws[1] that they use to walk safely on the ice and to catch their food. Polar bears are truly amazing animals.

[1]claws: sharp nails on the foot of an animal

ACTIVITY 7 | Choosing the best supporting sentence

Read each paragraph and the three possible supporting sentences below each paragraph. Then choose the best supporting sentence to complete the paragraph. Be prepared to explain your answer.

> **WORDS TO KNOW** Paragraphs 5.9 to 5.10
>
> **complicated:** (adj) difficult, complex   **current:** (adj) happening now

PARAGRAPH 5.9

Keeping Score in Tennis

Keeping score in tennis is a little **complicated**. To win a match, a player usually needs to win two sets. To win a set, a player needs to win six games before the other player does. Thus, a set score might be 6-2 or 6-4, for example. To win a game, a player has to win four points before the other player. In most sports, the points are numbered in a very simple and usual order: 1, 2, 3, etc. _____ However, in tennis, the first point in a game is 15, the second point is 30, and the third point is 40. The final point is simply called game.

a. Therefore, a typical match score might be 6-4, 6-2.

b. In baseball, for example, the first score is 1, the second is 2, etc.

c. The history of the game of tennis is also very complicated, so the scoring system is different.

Words with Many Meanings

Many high-frequency words are common because they have several meanings. For example, the word *take* can mean "to get with your hands" or "to use a bus." The word *book* can mean "something you read" or "to make a reservation for a trip." _____ Finally, the word **current** can mean "something that is happening now" or "the movement of air, water, or electricity." These four examples show why it can be difficult to learn common vocabulary in English.

a. The word *right* can mean "the opposite of left," but this same word also means "correct."

b. It is very easy to book a trip using a website available for travel searching.

c. Third, words can be spelled in several different ways.

Grammar: Articles

The **articles** *a*, *an*, and *the* can cause problems for English-language learners. Here are a few guidelines. See "Articles" in the *Writer's Handbook* for more information.

EXPLANATION	EXAMPLES
Use *a/an* before a <u>singular</u> <u>count noun</u> that is not specific. • Use *a* before a consonant sound. • Use *an* before a vowel sound.	My mother is **a** <u>teacher</u>. Many people believe *13* is **an** unlucky <u>number</u>.
Use *the* when talking about a specific singular or plural noun.	**The** test was difficult. I did not know **the** answers to **the** last five questions.
Do not use an article for nonspecific plural nouns or non-count nouns.	We ate steak, potatoes, and carrots. Would you like sugar in your tea?
Use *the* for the second (or subsequent) time you talk about something.	Flight 226 from Miami to Tokyo has a pilot and two copilots. **The** pilot has more than 10 years of experience, but **the** copilots have just a few.
Use *the* when you use a <u>superlative</u> form.	**The** <u>most</u> <u>interesting</u> movie was *The Hunger Games*.
Do not use an article with <u>abstract nouns</u>.	**Learning** is fun.
To talk about a category of things, use a <u>plural count noun</u> without *the*.	<u>Computers</u> are found in many American homes.

Compare:

✓ My mother is **a** teacher. *(general; answers What does your mother do?)*

✓ My mother is **the** teacher. *(specific; answers Who is the teacher of this class?)*

✓ **A** teacher walked into the room *(general; an unnamed or unknown person)*

✓ **The** teacher walked into the room. *(specific = our teacher or a known teacher)*

✓ Teachers are friendly. *(general = teachers everywhere)*

✓ **The** teachers are friendly. *(specific = the teachers at a particular school)*

ACTIVITY 8 | Using articles in a paragraph

Complete the paragraph with the correct article (or no article). Write *a*, *an*, *the*, or Ø (for no article).

> **WORDS TO KNOW** Paragraph 5.11
>
> **contest:** (n) a competition   **relative:** (n) a family member

PARAGRAPH 5.11

The Best Cook in the World

Without a doubt, my grandmother is [1] _____ best cook in world. Many people say that their mother or grandmother can cook [2] _____ spaghetti, [3] _____ fried fish, or [4] _____ beans really well. However, if there was a cooking **contest** right now, I am sure that my grandmother would win. My grandmother has cooked for 6 children, 15 grandchildren, 24 great-grandchildren, and many more **relatives** during her lifetime. My family lives in southern Louisiana, so my grandmother knows how to cook regional foods, such as [5] _____ seafood, [6] _____ red beans and rice, and gumbo, which is [7] _____ kind of seafood soup. Sometimes she uses [8] _____ cookbook, but most of the time she cooks from memory. Anyone who eats a plate of her fried chicken or [9] _____ meatballs will certainly agree that she is [10] _____ fantastic cook.

BUILDING BETTER VOCABULARY

> **WORDS TO KNOW**
>
> adapt (v) AW
> apply (v)
> attempt (v)
> available (adj) AW
> complicated (adj)
> contest (n)
> current (adj)
> former (adj)
>
> guard (v)
> harsh (adj)
> hide (v)
> increase (v)
> narrow (adj)
> ought to (aux v)
> pour (v)
> relative (n)
>
> remarkable (adj)
> score (v)
> site (n) AW
> spill (v)
> spot (n)
> spread (v)
> stir (v)
> submit (v) AW

ACTIVITY 9 | Word associations

Circle the word or phrase that is more closely related to the bold word on the left.

1. adapt	change	destroy
2. attempt	decide	try
3. contest	generation	winner
4. guard	believe	protect
5. hide	prevent from buying	prevent from seeing
6. narrow	not covered	not wide
7. pour	coffee or tea	bread or cake
8. remarkable	something bad	something good
9. spread	move	relax
10. stir	your lawn	your coffee

ACTIVITY 10 | Collocations

Fill in the blank with the word that most naturally completes the phrase.

apply	former	narrow	ought to	score

1. _____ for a new job

2. a _____ address

3. _____ eat more fruit

4. a _____ street

5. _____ 10 points in one game

contest	current	harsh	pour	site

6. _____ milk into a bowl

7. a _____ between two players

8. the best _____ for a new hospital

9. at the _____ time

10. very _____ weather

ACTIVITY 11 | Word forms

Complete each sentence with the correct word form. Use the correct forms of the words.

NOUN	VERB	ADJECTIVE	ADVERB	SENTENCES
application/ applicant	apply			**1.** Fill out an _____ if you want to be considered. **2.** Is it time for me to _____ for a new job?
attempt	attempt			**3.** The dancer_____ the new move several times before getting it right.
availability		available		**4.** This car is _____ in four different colors. **5.** The _____ of fresh water is limited in some countries.
complication	complicate	complicated		**6.** Taking two kinds of medicines might cause a _____ . **7.** The situation is very _____ .
relative	relate	related		**8.** English and German are _____ languages.
	remark	remarkable	remarkably	**9.** After their last game, the coach gave a truly _____ speech. **10.** _____ , no one was injured in yesterday's accident.

ACTIVITY 12 | Vocabulary in writing

Choose five words from Words to Know. Write a complete sentence with each word.

1. _____

_____

2. _____

_____

3. _____

_____

4. _____

_____

5. _____

_____

BUILDING BETTER SENTENCES

ACTIVITY 13 | Unscrambling sentences

Unscramble the words and phrases to write a complete sentence. More than one answer may be possible. Add commas where needed.

1. the University of Florida / Camilo Villegas is / who attended / a professional golf player

_____

_____

2. in the United States / not great / cat owners / the difference is / dog owners outnumber / but

_____

_____

3. foreign country / young people / to travel / many / to a / there are / reasons why / want

_____

_____

4. 28 university students / in this / I asked / dislikes regarding online exams / and / about / research project / their likes

_____

_____

5. of the country / were born / of / in / many / in the eastern part / U.S. history / the important people

_____

_____

A classmate wrote questions in the margin about her paragraph. Read the paragraph, answer the questions, and correct the mistakes. Find and correct five other mistakes. Check your answers with your class.

PARAGRAPH 5.12

The Florida Everglades

The Everglades region consists in a huge area of very
wet land that can be found only in southern Florida.
Water is extremely important to this unique environment
This area was formed by hundreds of years of flooding
from lake Okeechobee after heavy rains. These floods
always provided the land with new water for support its
wide variety of plants and animals. Unfortunately people
and nature are now taking away too much water from the
Everglades. For example the Miami River, Little River
and New River all take water away from the Everglades.
Even worse, man-made dams and canals prevents flooding,
without this flooding or other source of fresh water, the
everglades will die one day. Only time will tell whether this
unique area will survive. Or be lost forever.

consist in? consist of?

Water or The water?

Should I capitalize "lake"?

Is "for support" correct?

Do I need a comma after "Unfortunately"?

Do I need to put commas in this list of river names?

"prevents" or "prevent"?

"time" or "the time"?

Lake
Okeechobee

Miami

FLORIDA

Everglades
National Park

area
enlarged

ACTIVITY 15 | Combining sentences

Combine the ideas into one sentence. You may change the word forms, but do not change or omit any ideas. There may be more than one answer.

1. In this city, residents can find schools, housing, and transportation.
The transportation is convenient.
The schools are good, and the housing is affordable.
The residents are new.
The transportation is public.

_____

_____

2. Students can ask a former teacher to write a letter.
Students can ask a sports coach to write a letter.
Students can ask another adult to write a letter.
This occurs when the students are applying for a job.

_____

_____

3. A shot is worth two points.
This is a regular shot.
A shot is worth three points.
This is a longer shot.
This happens in basketball.

_____

_____

WRITING

ACTIVITY 16 | Writing a paragraph

Write a paragraph of five to ten sentences. Follow these guidelines:

1. Write about a place that you would like to visit (but have never been to).
2. Brainstorm what you could write about this place.
3. After you have chosen your ideas for your paragraph, write a topic sentence with a controlling idea.
4. After you write your paragraph, check to see if all the supporting sentences are related to the controlling idea in the topic sentence.

5. In your concluding sentence, restate the topic, offer a suggestion, give an opinion, or make a prediction.

6. Use at least two of the vocabulary words or phrases presented in Words to Know. Underline them in your paragraph.

ACTIVITY 17 | Peer editing

Work with a partner. Read your partner's paragraph from Activity 16. Use Peer Editing Form 5 in the *Writer's Handbook*. Offer positive suggestions to help your partner write a better paragraph. Consider your partner's comments as you revise your paragraph.

Additional Topics for Writing

Here are more ideas for writing a paragraph. When you write your paragraph, follow the directions for Activity 16.

TOPIC 1: Look at the photo at the beginning of the unit. Imagine you see these bears (or other wild animals) when you are on a walk. What emotions do you experience? What do you do?

TOPIC 2: What do you think will be the highest-paying occupation 50 years from now? Give reasons to support your opinion.

TOPIC 3: What is the definition of a perfect parent? What are the characteristics of such a person?

TOPIC 4: Choose a mechanical device, such as a watch, a coffee maker, or a smartphone. How does it work? Explain the process step by step.

TOPIC 5: The United Nations was formed in 1945 to promote world peace. However, some people think that the United Nations is not useful. Do you think the United Nations is useful? Explain.

TEST PREP

> ### TIP
>
> Avoid information that is too general. When possible, give specific examples. Good writers want to show that they have thought about the topic, and they should aim to provide interesting and specific information in their writing. For example, a sentence like "Cookies are not healthy." does not give the reader any new information. However, a sentence like this is more informative: "Research shows that the amount of sugar in cookies and other sweet treats can create a variety of health problems."

You should spend about 25 minutes on this task. Write a paragraph with 6–10 sentences.

What are the best snack foods for busy adults who care about their health?

Be sure to include a topic sentence, one or two strong supporting reasons for each of your choices, and a solid concluding sentence. Write at least 150 words.

6 | Definition Paragraphs

OBJECTIVES · Analyze a definition paragraph
· Cite exact words from a source
· Write sentences with adjective clauses
· Combine sentences to add variety to your writing
· Write a definition paragraph

A father and son in New Delhi, India, show the beautiful bond between two generations.

FREEWRITE | Look at the photo and read the caption. What do you think the word *bond* means? Write a definition in your own words.

ELEMENTS OF GREAT WRITING

What Is a Definition Paragraph?

A **definition paragraph** defines a word, a phrase, or an idea. A definition paragraph might define the word *gossip* and give examples. Another definition paragraph might define the phrase *a true friend* and give examples that help readers understand the phrase better.

A definition paragraph:
- explains what something is
- gives facts, details, and examples to make the definition clear to readers

In an essay, it is common to have one paragraph that defines a word or a phrase before the writer gets to his or her main points. For example, in an essay about the effects of gossip, the writer might use paragraph 2 to define the word *gossip*. Thus, a definition paragraph can be a very important part of a well-written essay.

ACTIVITY 1 | Analyzing a definition paragraph

Read the paragraph and answer the questions that follow.

WORDS TO KNOW Paragraph 6.1

destroy: (v) to ruin or put an end to
on purpose: (phr) not by accident

private: (adj) secret or personal
range: (v) to extend (from X to Y)

PARAGRAPH 6.1

Gossip

According to *The Newbury House Dictionary of American English*, gossip is "talk or writing about other people's actions or lives, sometimes untruthful." For example, if someone sees a friend crying, and then tells someone else that the friend was crying and has emotional problems, this is gossip. At first, gossip might not seem bad. One person tells a second person something **private** about someone else, and that second person tells a third, and so on. The information passes from person to person. However, gossip is much more than just information. The gossip can grow and change. People often do not know all the facts. They may add something untrue, either **on purpose** or not. As a result, the person who is the subject of the gossip may be hurt. Because the results **range** from making the person feel bad to **destroying** his or her career, gossip is much worse than just "talk or writing."

1. What is the topic sentence of Paragraph 6.1?

_____

_____

2. What is the writer's opinion about gossip? Begin your answer with *The writer believes that gossip…*

_____

_____

3. Do all the supporting sentences relate to the topic?   ☐ Yes   ☐ No

4. This paragraph is about gossip. What are other words or ideas that you could write a similar definition paragraph about?

_____

ACTIVITY 2 | Analyzing a definition paragraph

Discuss the questions with your classmates. Then read the paragraph on the next page and answer the questions that follow.

1. Look at the map. Where is Louisiana? What popular city is in this state?
2. What is *seafood*? Give three examples.
3. Describe a popular dish from your country or hometown.

> **WORDS TO KNOW** Paragraph 6.2
>
> **accurately:** (adv) correctly, precisely   **regional:** (adj) from one region or area
> **contain:** (v) to hold   **thick:** (adj) opposite of thin
> **regardless of:** (prep) no matter

Gumbo

The Newbury House Dictionary of American English defines gumbo as "a **thick** soup made with okra[1] and meat, fish, or vegetables," but anyone who has tasted this delicious dish knows that this definition is too simple to describe gumbo **accurately**. It is true that gumbo is a thick soup, but it is much more than that. Gumbo, which is one of the most popular of all Louisiana dishes, can be made with many different kinds of ingredients. For example, seafood gumbo usually **contains** shrimp and crab. Other kinds of gumbo can include chicken, sausage, or turkey. Three other important ingredients that all gumbo recipes use are okra, onions, and green peppers. **Regardless of** the ingredients in gumbo, this dish from the southern part of Louisiana is one of the most delicious **regional** foods in the United States.

[1]okra: a long green vegetable used in soups, stews, etc.

1. What is the topic sentence of this paragraph? _____

_____

_____

2. Do all the supporting sentences relate to the topic? ☐ Yes ☐ No

3. This paragraph is about gumbo. What are other topics that you could use to write a definition paragraph similar to this one?

_____

_____

Citing Exact Words from a Source

When you write, the ideas and the words are usually your own. However, sometimes you might want to borrow words from a source such as a book or a person. The action of mentioning or quoting a book, person, or other source is called **citing**.

When a **citation** is a direct quotation, be sure to put quotation marks ("…") around those words to show that the words are not yours. In addition, put commas, periods, and question marks that are part of the quote inside the quotation marks.

Here are three ways to write a definition with a direct quotation:

1. **According to** *The Newbury House Dictionary of American English*, gossip **is** "talk or writing about other people's actions or lives, sometimes untruthful."

2. *The Newbury House Dictionary of American English* **defines** gossip **as** "talk or writing about other people's actions or lives, sometimes untruthful."

3. **In** *The Newbury House Dictionary of American English*, gossip **is defined as** "talk or writing about other people's actions or lives, sometimes untruthful."

ACTIVITY 3 | Punctuating direct quotations

Add quotation marks, commas, and periods where necessary.

1. According to *The Newbury House Dictionary of American English*, an errand is a short trip made for a specific purpose

2. In *The Newbury House Dictionary of American English*, family is defined as one's closest relatives, usually parents, children, brothers, and sisters but the dictionary does not include grandparents or cousins.

3. *The Newbury House Dictionary of American English* defines stubborn as unwilling to change one's mind but is that always a bad thing?

4. According to *The Newbury House Dictionary of American English*, a fruit is the part of a plant that contains the seed, especially when used as food so a tomato is a fruit.

5. *The Newbury House Dictionary of American English* defines checkers as a game played by two people, each with 12 round black or red pieces (checkers) moved on a board divided into squares of two different colors but the game is much simpler than it sounds here.

Grammar: Adjective Clauses

One of the most common ways to write a definition is to use an adjective clause. An **adjective clause** describes a noun that comes before it. There are two main kinds of adjective clauses: subject adjective clauses and object adjective clauses.

Subject Adjective Clauses

Subject adjective clauses begin with a relative pronoun (*that, which, or who*) followed by a verb. The relative pronoun is the subject of the clause.

EXPLANATION	EXAMPLES
Use *that* or *which* for things. (*That* is more common.)	subject adjective clause Gumbo is a thick soup that contains seafood or meat. n rel v obj pron
Use *who* or *that* for people.	subject adjective clause A goalie is a player who protects the team's goal. n rel v obj pron

Object Adjective Clauses

Object adjective clauses begin with a relative pronoun (*that, which, who, or whom*) followed by a subject and a verb. The relative pronoun is the object of the verb in the clause.

EXPLANATION	EXAMPLES
Use *that* or *which* for things. (*That* is more common.)	object adjective clause Gumbo is a thick soup that people in Louisiana cook. n rel subj v pron
Use *whom* or *that* for people. In informal spoken English, *who* is often used for *whom*.	object adjective clause A goalie is a player who(m) the coach selects. n rel subj v pron

Notes:

The object relative pronoun can often be omitted.

✓ Gumbo is a thick soup (that) people in Louisiana cook.

✓ A goalie is a player (who/m) the coach selects.

The subject relative pronoun <u>cannot</u> be omitted.

✓ Gumbo is a thick soup <u>that</u> is popular in New Orleans.

✗ Gumbo is a thick <u>soup is</u> popular in New Orleans.

In an object relative clause, do not repeat the object.

✓ Gumbo is a thick soup that people in Louisiana <u>cook</u>.

✗ Gumbo is a thick soup that people in Louisiana <u>cook it</u>.

ACTIVITY 4 | Recognizing adjective clauses in a paragraph

Read the paragraph. Underline the five adjective clauses. Circle the noun that each clause describes. Tell a partner which are subject and which are object adjective clauses.

> **WORDS TO KNOW** Paragraph 6.3
>
> **entire:** (adj) whole
> **exceed:** (v) to be more than
> **flood:** (n) excess water covering land
> **in advance:** (phr) before
>
> **keep track of:** (phr v) to follow the most recent information about, or the location of something
> **region:** (n) an area
> **resident:** (n) a person who lives in a certain area

PARAGRAPH 6.3

Nature's Worst Storm

A hurricane is a dangerous (storm) that has high winds and heavy rain. Along coasts, the heavy rain often results in **floods** that destroy **entire** towns, and many hurricanes have winds that can **exceed** 100 miles per hour. Hurricane season in the Atlantic Ocean is between April and November. However, August and September are the months that people usually think of when they think of hurricanes. The worst hurricanes are usually in late summer and early fall. Modern technology now makes it possible for people who live on the coast to know **in advance** if there is the possibility of a hurricane hitting their **region**. However, this was not always the case. In 1900, for example, there was a hurricane in Galveston, Texas, that killed thousands of **residents**. Although we know much more about hurricanes now and can **keep track of** their movements, they continue to be one of the most dangerous weather events.

Palm trees in the wind and rain as Hurricane Irene makes landfall in August of 2011; Nassau, Bahamas

ACTIVITY 5 | Defining with subject adjective clauses

Write a new sentence with a subject adjective clause that defines the underlined word.

1. Brazil is a large <u>country</u>. Brazil covers about half of South America.

   Brazil is a large country <u>that covers about half of South America</u>.

2. The 737 is a commonly used <u>jet</u>. The 737 first flew in 1967.

   _____

3. A kindergarten teacher is a special <u>person</u>. A kindergarten teacher needs a lot of patience.

   _____

4. This paper will discuss a <u>beverage</u>. The beverage is made with coffee.

   _____

5. Bode Miller is an Olympic <u>skier</u>. This Olympic skier has won several medals.

   _____

6. Barack Obama was the U.S. <u>president</u>. Barack Obama started a national health plan in 2010.

   _____

ACTIVITY 6 | Defining with object adjective clauses

Write a new sentence with an object adjective clause at the end.

1. Orlando is a city in central Florida. Millions of tourists visit Orlando each year.

   Orlando is a city in central Florida <u>that millions of tourists visit each year</u>.

2. Coffee is a popular beverage. Many people drink it several times every day.

   _____

3. Winston Churchill is a famous person. Historians remember him for his strong leadership.

   _____

4. Algebra is a complicated subject. Some students do not like this subject.

   _____

5. Good writing includes clear definitions. Readers can easily understand these definitions.

   _____

6. The quarter is a U.S. coin. The government first made this coin in 1796.

   _____

A gopher tortoise, an endangered species found in the southeastern United States

ACTIVITY 7 | Writing definitions with adjective clauses

Write a definition for each word, phrase, place, or name. Write a subject adjective clause for 1–4, and an object adjective clause for 5–8.

1. tortoise: _A tortoise is a slow-moving animal that goes inside its hard shell when there is danger._

2. copilot: _____

_____

3. passport: _____

_____

4. submarine: _____

_____

5. odd numbers: _____

_____

6. plumber: _____

_____

7. Serena Williams: _____

_____

8. the United Nations: _____

_____

Grammar: Sentence Variety

Many beginning writers use only simple sentences that have a subject, a verb, and an object. You can improve your paragraphs by using different kinds of sentences. Here are three ways to create sentence variety.

Combining Sentences with Conjunctions

For variety, combine two simple sentences with a conjunction (connector). See the *Writer's Handbook* for more information on connectors.

> The scientist forgot to control the temperature. The experiment was not successful.

> The scientist forgot to control the temperature, **so** the experiment was not successful.

Combining Sentences with Adjectives and Adjective Clauses

In addition to connecting words, you can use adjectives and adjective clauses for variety.

> The students liked the professor's suggestion.

> Adjectives: The **international** students liked the professor's **creative** suggestion.

> Adjective Clauses: The students **who study ESL** liked the suggestion **that the professor made**.

Combining Sentences with Prepositional Phrases

You can also use prepositional phrases for variety.

> I did all the homework.

> I did all the homework **in about three hours**.

ACTIVITY 8 | Comparing writing with and without sentence variety

Work with a partner. Read the short paragraphs and answer the questions that follow.

> I was walking on Stern Street. I was in front of the bank. I heard a bang. It was loud. The front door of the bank opened. This happened suddenly. A man left the bank. He did this hurriedly. He was tall. He had wavy hair. It was brown. He had a gun. It was shiny. It was in his right hand.

> I was walking in front of the bank on Stern Street. Suddenly I heard a loud bang, and the front door of the bank opened. A tall man who had wavy brown hair hurriedly left the bank. In his right hand, he had a shiny gun.

1. How many sentences are in Example 1? _____ Example 2? _____

2. What differences do you notice in the writing styles? Which do you prefer? Explain.

_____

_____

ACTIVITY 9 | Sentence combining

Combine the ideas to write a supporting sentence for Paragraph 6.4. Then read the paragraph and check (✓) the place in the paragraph where the sentence fits best.

People used pottery. ~~This was in ancient times.~~	The pottery was made of clay. The pottery was for plates.	The pottery was for bowls.

In ancient times,

_____

WORDS TO KNOW Paragraph 6.4

careless: (adj) not caring about details
expert: (n) a person who knows a subject very well
occasionally: (adv) sometimes

related: (adj) connected with
respected: (adj) describes someone or something that others think highly of

---

PARAGRAPH 6.4

An Unusual Word Relationship

You might never guess that the word *sincere* is **related** to making pottery. [1] _____ Some language **experts** say that *sincere* comes from two Latin words: *sin* meaning "without" and *cero* meaning "wax[1]." Thus, *sincere* means "without wax." [2] _____ It took a long time to make this pottery. **Occasionally,** the pottery had cracks in it and was not good quality.

[3] _____ Some potters who did not want to make brand-new pottery put wax on the crack to cover the mistake. To the eye of a **careless** shopper, the pottery looked good. However, people soon realized which potters were good and which were not. Thus, the most **respected** potters made pottery that was without wax, or "sincere," and that is how the word *sincere* came to mean honest or truthful in thoughts and actions. [4] _____

[1]wax: the material that candles are made of

Ancient Roman pottery with cracks

BUILDING BETTER VOCABULARY

WORDS TO KNOW

accurately (adv) AW	flood (n)	regardless of (prep)
careless (adj)	in advance (phr)	region (n) AW
contain (v)	keep track (of) (phr v)	regional (adj) AW
destroy (v)	occasionally (adv)	related (adj)
entire (adj)	on purpose (phr)	resident (n) AW
exceed (v) AW	private (adj)	respected (adj)
expert (n) AW	range (v) AW	thick (adj)

ACTIVITY 10 | Word associations

Circle the word or phrase that is more closely related to the bold word or phrase on the left.

1. accurately	count	laugh
2. contain	give	have
3. flood	too much money	too much water
4. keep track of	follow	try
5. occasionally	sometimes	today's event
6. on purpose	immediately	not by accident
7. regardless of	in spite of	instead of
8. region	area of land	number of people
9. related	connected	memorized
10. thick	water	gumbo

ACTIVITY 11 | Collocations

Fill in the blank with the word that most naturally completes the phrase.

careless	exceed	range	related	track

1. _____ 200

2. their ages _____ from 18 to 24

3. to keep _____ of my appointments

4. _____ to someone

5. _____ drivers

advance	entire	private	resident	respected

6. a long-time _____ of New York

7. a _____ meeting

8. a _____ leader

9. apologize in _____

10. the _____ year

ACTIVITY 12 | Word forms

Complete each sentence with the correct word form. Use the correct forms of the words.

NOUN	VERB	ADJECTIVE	ADVERB	SENTENCES
accuracy		accurate	accurately	**1.** The _____ of the data is in question. **2.** If you answer 8 questions _____, you will pass the test.
carelessness		careless	carelessly	**3.** Children are often _____ with their things. **4.** Her _____ was the reason she got fired.
expert expertise		expert	expertly	**5.** Her _____ was in mathematics. **6.** He is an _____ in the field.
occasion		occasional	occasionally	**7.** We _____ have heavy rain in July, but it is not usual. **8.** Today is a special _____ for Paul.
resident residence	reside	residential		**9.** The plan is for this to be a _____ area. **10.** How many people _____ in this house?

ACTIVITY 13 | Vocabulary in writing

Choose five words from Words to Know. Write a sentence with each word.

1. _____

_____

2. _____

_____

3. _____

_____

4. _____

_____

5. _____

_____

BUILDING BETTER SENTENCES

ACTIVITY 14 | Scrambled sentences in a paragraph

Unscramble the three groups of words to create the three missing sentences for the paragraph "Patience." Then write the sentences in the correct place in the paragraph.

1. patience / with young children / see / who works / we / in a teacher / can

_____

_____

2. people / unfortunately, in / lack / our modern society, / often / simple patience

_____

_____

3. is difficult / the ability / even when a situation / I define / to stay calm / patience as

_____

_____

Patience

Patience means the ability to continue doing something even if you do not see any results right away. [1] _____

_____

The teacher repeats things many times and does not get angry when a child does not listen immediately. We can see patience in a clerk who treats a customer politely even though the clerk has already been working with other customers for seven or eight hours. We can see patience in a person who is waiting in line at the grocery store on a very busy day. [2] _____.

_____

People nowadays expect immediate results all the time. [3] _____

_____

ACTIVITY 15 | Editing

Find and correct the seven errors in this paragraph. The errors are: missing commas (2), missing subject (1), verb tense (2), missing article (1), and word form (1).

Seward's Folly

A folly is a foolish act that has a bad or a very strange result. Alaska was called "Seward's Folly" because Secretary of State William Seward convince Congress to buy Alaska from Russia. Alaska is now the largest oil-producing state in the United States, but buying it from Russia in 1867 was then considered a foolish act. At that time, many Americans think that it was waste of money. However they were wrong. Large amounts of gold and other minerals have been found in Alaska. Alaska is also important because produces oil for the United States. Perhaps the purchase of Alaska in 1867 seemed like a bad decision at the time but today we know that buy Alaska was certainly not a folly.

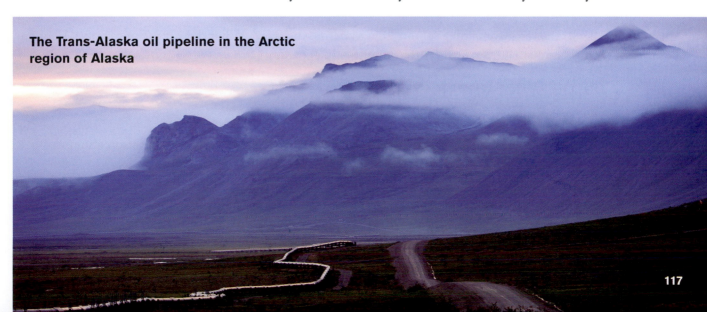

The Trans-Alaska oil pipeline in the Arctic region of Alaska

ACTIVITY 16 | Combining sentences

Combine the ideas into one sentence. You may change the word forms, but do not change or omit any ideas. There may be more than one correct answer.

1. Abraham Lincoln was the president.
   He worked to save the country.
   This was during the Civil War.

   _____

   _____

2. A sentence has two subjects.
   A sentence has two verbs.
   A sentence might be a compound sentence.

   _____

   _____

3. I will discuss the reasons.
   This will happen in this paper.
   In this city, residents cannot find cheap housing.
   In this city, residents cannot find cheap transportation.

   _____

   _____

WRITING

ACTIVITY 17 | Writing a paragraph

Write a definition paragraph. Follow these guidelines.

1. Choose one of these words to define: *love*, *respect*, or *fear*.

2. Brainstorm some ideas about how to define the word. What does it mean to you? What are examples, stories, or facts that might help explain it?

3. Write a topic sentence with a controlling idea.

4. Write supporting sentences that relate to the topic.

5. End with a concluding sentence that restates the topic or makes a prediction about it.

6. If you use words from another source, put quotation marks around them.

7. Use at least two of the vocabulary words or phrases presented in Words to Know.

8. If you need help, study the example definition paragraphs in this unit.

ACTIVITY 18 | Peer editing

Work with a partner. Read your partner's paragraph from Activity 17. Then use Peer Editing Form 6 in the *Writer's Handbook*. Be sure to offer positive suggestions to help your partner write a better paragraph. Consider your partner's comments as you revise your paragraph.

Additional Topics for Writing

Here are more ideas for definition paragraphs. When you write your paragraph, follow the guidelines in Activity 17.

TOPIC 1: Look at the photo at the beginning of the unit. Consider the photo and write a paragraph in which you define *family*. Use your own ideas and experience as well.

TOPIC 2: Choose a scientific or medical term, such as *gravity*, *tsunami*, *molecule*, *appendix*, or *pediatrics*. What is it? Why is it important?

TOPIC 3: Write a paragraph in which you define the word *pride*. What is it? What is its purpose? When should people feel pride?

TOPIC 4: Write about a word or phrase that is borrowed from another language. Examples of borrowed words in English are *robot*, *siesta*, and *sushi*. What language does the word or phrase come from? What does the word or phrase mean in that language? Is the meaning the same in English?

TOPIC 5: What is freedom? Why do people want it? Should everyone have it without limits? What limits should there be (if any)? Explain.

TEST PREP

You should spend about 25 minutes on this task. Write a paragraph with 6–10 sentences.

What does the word courage *mean to you? Give examples to help your readers better understand your definition.*

Be sure to include a topic sentence, strong supporting sentences with examples or reasons, and a solid concluding sentence. Write at least 150 words.

> **TIP**
> Organize your ideas. Review the notes you brainstorm and number each idea from most important to least important. Choose the ideas you want to write about. Write the most important supporting idea last.

7 | Process Paragraphs

Researchers in survival suits measure the contents of the ice and water. This allows them to track changes over time. Canada Basin, Arctic Ocean

FREEWRITE | Look at the photo and read the caption. List any steps you think are necessary to prepare for a trip to the Arctic.

ELEMENTS OF GREAT WRITING

What Is a Process Paragraph?

A **process paragraph** explains how to do something. In a process paragraph, you divide a process into separate steps. You list or explain the steps in chronological order—the order of events as they happen over time. Special time words or phrases allow you to tell the reader the sequence of the steps. The process paragraph ends with a specific result—something that happens at the end of the process.

In this type of paragraph, the writer sometimes uses the imperative form (*First,* **sit down.** *Next,* **open your book.**) Another option is to use *you* or *we*: *First,* **you put** *your credit card into the card reader. Next,* **you enter** *your four-digit PIN.*

In summary, a process paragraph:
- explains a sequence or process
- presents facts and details in chronological order
- uses time words or phrases such as *first, second, after that,* and *last*
- ends with a specified result

You can use a frame like this to help organize a process paragraph.

Topic Sentence	_____
Step 1	_____
Step 2	_____
Step 3	_____
Concluding Sentence	_____

ACTIVITY 1 | Analyzing a process paragraph

Discuss the questions with your classmates. Then read the paragraph and answer the questions that follow.

1. Can you give an example of a dish from Mexico? If so, what is it? What ingredients do you need to make it?
2. What is a food that is messy to eat? How do you eat it?

WORDS TO KNOW Paragraph 7.1

at an angle: (phr) not straight; leans to a side
embarrassing: (adj) causing an uncomfortable feeling due to a difficult or confusing situation

messy: (adj) not neat or clean
slight: (adj) small

PARAGRAPH 7.1

Messy Food

Eating a delicious, juicy taco is **messy**, so it is important to know how to eat one. First, be sure that you are wearing clothes that you can get dirty. Eating a taco while you are wearing an expensive shirt or other clothing is not a good idea. Next, decide if you want to eat the taco in front of the person you are with. Eating a taco in front of someone you do not know well can be **embarrassing**. Then, to eat the taco, pick it up, but be careful not to spill the ingredients. As you raise the taco, slowly turn your head toward it and position your head **at a slight angle**. The last step is to put the corner of the taco in your mouth and take a bite. By following these simple directions, you will stay clean as you eat this delicious food.

1. What is the topic sentence of Paragraph 7.1?

   _____

   _____

2. What are four steps to take when eating a taco?

   1. _____

   2. _____

   3. _____

   4. _____

3. Do you think that the writer wants this paragraph to be serious, angry, or funny? Explain.

   _____

ACTIVITY 2 | Analyzing a process paragraph

Discuss the questions with your classmates. Then read the paragraph and answer the questions that follow.

1. What is your favorite strategy for increasing your English vocabulary?
2. Do you keep a vocabulary notebook of new English words? Explain.

> **WORDS TO KNOW** Paragraph 7.2
>
> **assume:** (v) to suppose
> **likely:** (adj) probable
> **organized:** (adj) arranged in a certain way
>
> **translation:** (n) words that have been changed from one language to another

---

PARAGRAPH 7.2

Keeping a Vocabulary Notebook

Keeping a vocabulary notebook for learning new English words is not complicated if you follow a few easy steps. First, buy a notebook with at least 100 lined pages. You should select the color and size notebook that you prefer. Second, write down any important words that you come across when reading or listening. This step requires you to decide whether a word is important enough for you to learn. Do not **assume** that you will remember the word later. The next step is a bit difficult because you need to decide what information about each word you will write in your notebook. Some learners write only a **translation** of the word. Others write an example phrase using the word. Include information that matches your learning style and your needs. Finally, the most important thing you can do to learn the words in your notebook is to practice these words several times. If the pages of your notebook are well **organized**, you are more **likely** to review the words and their information over and over. If you follow these important steps in keeping a good vocabulary notebook, you can improve your English greatly.

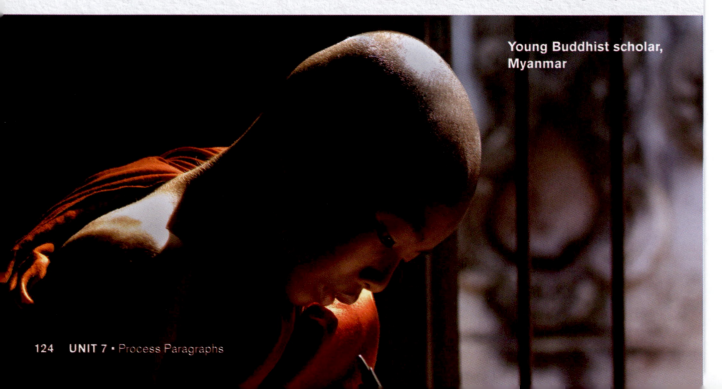

Young Buddhist scholar, Myanmar

1. What is the topic sentence of the paragraph?

   _____

   _____

2. Underline the sentences that introduce each of the four steps.

3. Does the paragraph explain the difference between the vocabulary you learn when reading and the vocabulary you learn when speaking? Explain.

   _____

   _____

4. According to the paragraph, what "three pieces of information" can you put in your notebook for each word?

   _____

   _____

   _____

Sequencing and Chronological Order

To show chronological order in a process, writers use various structures.

STRUCTURE	EXAMPLES	EXAMPLE SENTENCES
Transition words and phrases.	First, Second, Next, In addition, Then Finally,	**First,** you must buy a notebook with at least 100 pages. **Finally,** be sure to practice your new words every day.
Subject phrases	The first step (is to)… The last step (is to)…	**The last step** is to put the corner of the taco in your mouth and take a bite.
Clauses beginning with *before, after, the next thing (that)…, the last thing (that)…*	After you finish step one, the next thing you should do (is)…	**After you finish your first taco,** you can prepare for next one. **The next thing you should do** is decide if you want to eat the taco in front of others.

ACTIVITY 3 | Sequencing instructions

Look at the photos and tell a partner how you might explain the process of serving a tennis ball. Then read the sentences and order the remaining steps (2 to 7).

> **WORDS TO KNOW** Activity 3
>
> **peak:** (n) the highest point
> **position:** (n) location, place
>
> **reach:** (v) to move or stretch your hands out
> **substitute:** (v) to put something in place of another

1. _____ Hit the ball into the small box on the opposite side of the net.

2. _____ After you hit the ball, continue swinging your racket down and across the front of your body.

3. _____ Just before the ball **reaches** its **peak**, begin to swing your racket forward as high as you can.

4. _____ First, use your left hand to throw the ball about three feet in the air. The best **position** for the ball is just to the right of your head.

5. _____ At the same time, move your racket behind your shoulder with your right hand so that your elbow is pointed toward the sky.

6. _____ After you have completed the serve, your racket should be near your left knee.

7. __1__ Many people think serving in tennis is difficult, but the following steps show that it is quite easy. If you are left-handed, you should **substitute** the word *left* for *right* in these directions.

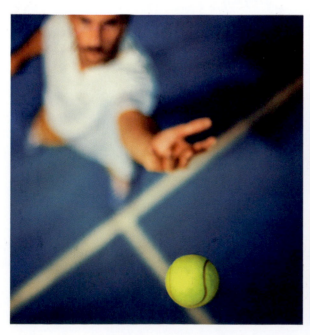

ACTIVITY 4 | Sequencing information in paragraph form

Write the sentences from Activity 3 in paragraph form. Give the process paragraph a title. Underline the sequence words.

_____

_____

_____

_____

_____

_____

_____

_____

_____

ACTIVITY 5 | Writing about a process you know

Use the paragraph you wrote in Activity 4 as a model to write a paragraph on a separate piece of paper about a process you know. For example, write about making an easy meal (a sandwich, toast, etc.), taking a photo, or fixing a flat tire. Then share it with a partner.

WRITER'S NOTE Using Note Cards to Help You Organize

It is important that all the steps in a process paragraph are in the correct order. A simple way for you to organize the steps is to write each one on a small card. This organization method will allow you to arrange and rearrange the steps. It will also help point out any steps that may be missing.

ACTIVITY 6 | Describing a process using math

Discuss the questions with your classmates. Then read the paragraph and answer the questions that follow.

1. Describe a magic trick that you saw someone do. Who was it? What did the person do? Do you know the secret of the trick?
2. Can you do a magic trick? If so, describe the trick or do it for your class.

WORDS TO KNOW Paragraph 7.3

divide: (v) to separate into equal parts
impressed: (adj) causing others to admire
multiply: (v) to increase a number by a certain number of times for a result

no matter: (phr) used to say that something is not important
original: (adj) the first or oldest
select: (v) to choose

Math or Magic?

This math trick will amaze your friends. Your friends choose any number they want, and then they all do the same math problem. **No matter** which number they **select**, their answer will always be 3. First, tell your friends to think of a number greater than zero (e.g., 5). Next, they should **multiply** their number by itself (5 x 5 = 25). After that, they should add their answer to their **original** number (25 + 5 = 30). Now they should **divide** their new total by their original number (30 ÷ 5 = 6). In the last steps, your friends should add 17 (6 + 17 = 23) and then subtract their original number from this last total (23 − 5 = 18). Finally, they should divide their answer by six (18 ÷ 6 = 3). The final result is always 3. Try it on your friends. They are sure to be **impressed**!

1. What are the first three steps in this math trick? Write them here. Circle any sequence words or phrases.

   (First,) tell your friends to think of a number greater than zero. _____

   _____

   _____

2. This process has many small steps. Good writers sometimes combine two or more steps into a longer sentence. Find and write the sentence that has more than one step in it.

   _____

   _____

   _____

3. Choose two steps and combine them into one sentence. Then share your sentence with a partner.

   _____

   _____

   _____

Grammar: The Imperative

Imperative sentences give directions or commands.

EXPLANATION	EXAMPLES
Use the base form of the verb to begin an imperative sentence. Note there is no subject in this form. The subject is understood as 'you.'	**Mix** these ingredients well.
Imperative sentences are common in writing that tells the reader how to do something.	To determine whether fire needs air, **do** a simple experiment with a small candle and a jar with a lid. **Place** the candle in the jar. **Light** the candle. Then **put** the lid on the jar.

ACTIVITY 7 | Using sequence expressions and the imperative

Complete the paragraph with the imperative form of the verb in parentheses. Add a possible sequence word or phrase where indicated (Seq). More than one sequence word is possible.

> **WORDS TO KNOW** Paragraph 7.4
>
> **alive:** (adj) living
> **empty:** (adj) having nothing inside
> **escape:** (v) to get out of a difficult situation or place
>
> **experiment:** (n) a test to see if something works
> **produce:** (v) to make or create
> **prove:** (v) to show to be true

PARAGRAPH 7.4

A goldfish in a jar

A Simple Experiment

Here is a simple science **experiment**. It **proves** that plants **produce** oxygen. This experiment requires a clean jar with a tight lid, some tape, a goldfish, some water, and a few green plants. [1] _____ (Seq/put) the water and the plants in the jar. When you do this, [2] _____ (be) sure to leave about an inch of **empty** space. When the water in the jar is at room temperature, [3] _____ (add) the fish to the jar. Put the lid on tightly. [4] _____ (Seq/wrap) the lid with several pieces of tape so that no air can pass through it, and [5] _____ (place) the jar in a cool place indoors. But be sure that it receives some direct sunlight for a few hours each day. [6] _____ (check) the fish regularly to be sure it stays healthy. (Remove the fish immediately if it looks sick.) The fish will still be **alive** even after a week. This shows that oxygen was added by the plants. If you look carefully at a plant in sunlight, you can see tiny bubbles of oxygen **escaping** from it.

BUILDING BETTER VOCABULARY

WORDS TO KNOW

alive (adj)	impressed (adj)	position (n)
assume (v) **AW**	likely (adj)	produce (v)
at an angle (phr)	messy (adj)	prove (v)
divide (v)	multiply (v) **AW**	reach (v)
embarrassing (adj)	no matter (phr)	select (v) **AW**
empty (adj)	organized (adj)	slight (adj)
escape (v)	original (adj)	substitute (v) **AW**
experiment (n)	peak (n)	translation (n) **AW**

ACTIVITY 8 | Word associations

Circle the word or phrase that is more closely related to the bold word or phrase on the left.

1. alive	sleeping	breathing
2. divide	8 ÷ 4 = 2	8 x 4 = 32
3. escape	leave a place	travel to a place
4. likely	friendly	possible
5. messy	not neat	not original
6. original	the first	the last
7. the peak	the lowest point	the highest point
8. position	time	place
9. produce	find	make
10. prove	show	try

ACTIVITY 9 | Collocations

Fill in the blank with the word that most naturally completes the phrase.

divide	embarrassing	messy	original	reach

1. the most _____ moment in my life

2. a very _____ room

3. hard to _____ the top shelf

4. _____ something between two people

5. the _____ price

| assume | experiment | select | slight | substitute |

6. a science _____

7. _____ that something is correct

8. _____ the best answer on the test

9. only a _____ difference between the two colors

10. _____ one ingredient for another

ACTIVITY 10 | Word forms

Complete each sentence with the correct word form. Use the correct forms of the words.

NOUN	VERB	ADJECTIVE	ADVERB	SENTENCES
assumption	assume			**1.** Let's _____ that his story is true.
embarrassment	embarrass	embarrassed embarrassing		**2.** Tim was _____ by what his professor said to him. **3.** How do most people react in an _____ situation?
		slight	slightly	**4.** Dishes from Argentina are only _____ spicy. **5.** The speaker had just a _____ French accent.
organization	organize	organized		**6.** The _____ of the essay is great. **7.** The writing in the third paragraph is not well _____. **8.** You should _____ your ideas before you write.
originality	originate	original	originally	**9.** What was the president's _____ answer? **10.** _____ , very few people agreed with his opinion.

131

ACTIVITY 11 | Vocabulary in writing

Choose five words from Words to Know. Write a complete sentence with each word.

1. _____
   _____

2. _____
   _____

3. _____
   _____

4. _____
   _____

5. _____
   _____

BUILDING BETTER SENTENCES

ACTIVITY 12 | Scrambled sentences

Order these groups of words to write a correct sentence. Use every word and do not add any words. More than one answer may be possible. Add commas where needed.

1. you completely / writing assignment / first, make sure / directions for the / understand the
   _____
   _____

2. appropriate for / a topic / the assignment / select / that is
   _____
   _____

3. brainstorm suitable / next, / or with / a partner / ideas alone
   _____
   _____

4. you have an / write an / after / appropriate topic, / outline of the assignment
   _____
   _____

5. with someone else and / share your outline / person's suggestions / then consider that
   _____
   _____

ACTIVITY 13 | Editing

Each sentence has (x) number of errors. Find and correct them.

1. First make sure that all of the sentences in the paragraph has a verb. (2)

2. When you are ready for purchase your ticket enter your credit card number. (2)

3. There have several steps you should to take to protect your information in the Internet. (3)

4. To answer a multiple-choice question, reading all of the choices before choose your answer. (2)

5. Finally save your information before you close a file, because your computer may not to save it automatically. (3)

ACTIVITY 14 | Combining sentences

Combine the ideas into one sentence. You may change the word forms, but do not change or omit any ideas. There may be more than one answer.

1. Add the onions.
Add the tomato slices.
Add the pepper.
Add these ingredients to the spinach.
It is the spinach that you just cooked.
The onions are chopped, and the pepper is black.
All of this is what you do second.

_____

_____

2. You should call the airline.
You should do this to see if they have already put you on another flight.
You should do this if your flight is canceled.

_____

_____

3. Tourists go through immigration.
Tourists must do this first.
Then tourists collect their bags.
Finally, they go through customs.
All of this occurs when tourists arrive in the United States.

_____

_____

WRITING

ACTIVITY 15 | Writing a paragraph

Write a process paragraph. Follow these guidelines.

1. Choose a topic for a process paragraph. Write about something you know how to do (e.g., a sport, a food you can make, something else you can make). Write a title and some notes about the steps in the process. Use the paragraph outline below.

2. Write your paragraph. Write a topic sentence with a clear controlling idea.

3. Write supporting sentences that give the steps in chronological order. Use correct words and structures to show that the steps are in the correct chronological order.

4. Use at least two of the vocabulary words or phrases in Words to Know. Underline these words and phrases in your paragraph.

_____(title)

Topic Sentence	_____
Step 1	_____
Step 2	_____
Step 3	_____
Concluding Sentence	_____

Work with a partner. Read your partner's paragraph from Activity 15. Then use Peer Editing Form 7 in the *Writer's Handbook*. Be sure to offer positive suggestions to help your partner write a better paragraph. Consider your partner's comments as you revise your paragraph.

Additional Topics for Writing

Here are more ideas for process paragraphs. When you write your paragraph, follow the guidelines in Activity 15.

TOPIC 1: Look at the photo at the beginning of the unit. Think about the steps you discussed to prepare for a trip to the Arctic. Then write about a trip you want to go on. What do you need to do to prepare for it?

TOPIC 2: Write about the steps in writing a good paragraph. How do you start? What information do you include?

TOPIC 3: Write about the steps a successful job applicant should follow. Where do you start? What resources do you use?

TOPIC 4: Write about what you need to do to get a driver's license.

TOPIC 5: Describe how to find the best price for something.

TEST PREP

You should spend about 25 minutes on this task. Write a paragraph with 6–10 sentences.

What should you do if the server at a restaurant gives you your check and it has a mistake on it? What are the steps you take to correct the error?

Be sure to include a topic sentence, clear steps in the process, and a concluding sentence. Use appropriate structures to show sequence. Use the imperative when giving the steps of the process. Write at least 150 words.

> **TIP**
> Write the concluding sentence last. Readers are more interested in the ideas and support you present than in your concluding sentence. If you do not have time to finish, it is better to leave out the concluding sentence than to leave out supporting sentences.

8 | Opinion Paragraphs

OBJECTIVES
- Analyze an opinion paragraph
- Distinguish between facts and opinions
- Recognize word forms and common suffixes
- Develop ideas for an opinion paragraph
- Write an opinion paragraph

A small seahorse holds a plastic swab in polluted waters near Sumbawa Besar, Sumbara Island, Indonesia. Seahorses travel through the ocean by holding floating objects with their tails.

FREEWRITE | Look at the photo and read the caption. What do you think about this photo? How does it make you feel? Explain.

ELEMENTS OF GREAT WRITING

What Is an Opinion Paragraph?

An **opinion paragraph** expresses the writer's thoughts about an issue. The writer presents an argument for or against something. In this type of writing, the writer often wants to get readers to have the same opinion or to change their opinion.

A well-written opinion paragraph includes facts to support the opinion. For example, if the topic sentence is "I believe smoking should not be allowed anywhere," the rest of the paragraph must give reasons for this opinion. One reason could be a fact, such as:

According to the CDC, 443,000 people in the United States die each year from diseases related to smoking.

This fact clearly and strongly supports the writer's opinion.

An opinion paragraph:

- is often about an issue people do not agree on
- gives the writer's opinion about the issue
- includes facts to support the writer's opinion
- often includes a citation, or note, to identify the source of these facts
- sometimes discusses the opposing opinion about the issue
- presents a strong case that makes the reader think about the issue seriously

ACTIVITY 1 | Analyzing an opinion paragraph

Discuss the questions with your classmates. Then read Paragraph 8.1 and answer the questions that follow.

1. Do you think that using a cell phone while driving is acceptable? Why or why not?
2. Should there be laws against the use of cell phones while driving? Why or why not?

PARAGRAPH 8.1

Driving and Cell Phones

Because talking on cell phones while driving is dangerous, every country should **prohibit** cell phone use by drivers. The most obvious reason for this **ban** is to save lives. According to the Centers for Disease Control and Prevention (CDC), each day in the United States, nine people are killed and over 1,000 are **injured** because they were talking on cell phones or texting while driving. As if the first reason is not enough, a second reason is that these drivers cause accidents that kill other people. Sometimes these drivers kill other drivers; sometimes they kill passengers or even pedestrians. These drivers do not have the right to endanger other people's lives. Finally, even in cases where there are no injuries or deaths, **damage** to cars from these accidents costs millions of dollars. To me, prohibiting cell phones while driving is **common sense**. This ban is already in effect in more than 30 countries, including Australia, Brazil, Japan, Russia, and Turkey. Other countries should do the same. We must all be careful drivers. Talking or texting on a cell phone while driving is not safe. For the important reasons given here, I support a complete ban on all cell phone use by drivers worldwide.

1. What is the purpose of this paragraph? Begin with *The purpose of this paragraph is to . . .* *what they are doing,*

   The purpose of this paragraph is to give to the readers a complete explanation with the facts about the importance of the Drivers, Do not

2. What opinion does the writer state in the topic sentence of the paragraph? *use the cell phone*

   The drivers do not use his cellphone won they driving.

3. What three reasons does the writer give to support this opinion?

   - *Each day in the United States nine people are killed on over . .*
   - *This drivers cause accident that kill other people.*
   - *The damage to cars from these accidents costs millions of dollars.*

4. What is a possible reason *not* to ban cell phone use when driving? Start with *Some people may believe . . . because . . .*

   Some people may believe that use the cell phone went driving it is safe because they use the cell phone whice a tools; GPS.

ACTIVITY 2 | Analyzing an opinion paragraph

Discuss the questions with your classmates. Then read Paragraph 8.2 and answer the questions that follow.

1. How many phone calls do you make each day? How many text messages do you send?
2. When you need to tell a person something, do you prefer to call or text that person? Why?

WORDS TO KNOW Paragraph 8.2

interact: (v) to communicate with someone through conversation, looks, or action

old-fashioned: (adj) old style, not modern
versus: (prep) in contrast to (also written *vs.*)

PARAGRAPH 8.2

Texting Versus Calling

Texting **versus** calling; which is better? Many of my friends try to convince me that I should text them more often, but I prefer calling to texting. Yes, some people might say that using a telephone to make a call is **old-fashioned**, but I do not care. Texting is certainly very common now because it is convenient and fast. However, I prefer to call my friends because I want to hear their voices and **interact** with them. Additionally, it is difficult to type while walking. It is much easier to speak. Without a doubt, calling is my preferred way of communicating.

1. What is the purpose of this paragraph? Begin with *The purpose of this paragraph is to . . .*

_____

2. What opinion does the writer state in the topic sentence of this paragraph?

_____

3. What phrases from the paragraph show that the writer is giving an opinion and not a fact?

_____

4. What sentence shows the other side of the issue? Underline it.

5. On a separate piece of paper, write two additional reasons to support each opinion.

ACTIVITY 3 | Writing an opinion paragraph

Write a paragraph similar to Paragraph 8.2, but with the opposite opinion (texting is better than calling). State this opinion in the topic sentence. Write two to three reasons to support this opinion.

ACTIVITY 4 | Analyzing an opinion paragraph

Discuss the questions with your classmates. Then read Paragraph 8.3 and answer the questions that follow.

1. Have you ever worn a school uniform?
2. Do you think requiring students to wear a uniform is a good idea or a bad idea?

WORDS TO KNOW Paragraph 8.3

benefit: (n) a good result of something
concentrate: (v) to think hard about something
freedom: (n) the ability to act without restriction

mandatory: (adj) describes something that must be done
waste time: (phr) to not use time wisely; spend time doing unimportant things

---

PARAGRAPH 8.3

An A+ for School Uniforms

In my opinion, school uniforms should be **mandatory** for all students. First of all, uniforms make everyone equal. In this way, kids with a lot of nice things can be on the same level as those with fewer things. In addition, parents and children know that getting ready for school every morning is much faster and easier if the school requires uniforms. Many kids **waste time** choosing what to wear to school, and they or their parents are often unhappy with their final choice. When I was in school, it only took me a few minutes to get dressed in my uniform. Finally, I believe that school uniforms make students work harder. When I wore my uniform in school, I **concentrated** more and got better grades. Some people might say that uniforms take away personal **freedom**, but students still have many other ways to express themselves. For all these reasons, I believe the **benefits** of school uniforms are so strong that we should require them immediately.

1. What is the author's opinion about school uniforms?

_____

2. The author gives three reasons to support the opinion. Write them here.

_____

_____

_____

3. The paragraph states that some people do not think that school uniforms should be required. What is their main reason? Discuss the reason as a class.

ACTIVITY 5 | Sequencing sentences

Read the eight types of sentences in a paragraph. Then read the sentences below and match them (2 to 8) to their purpose in the paragraph.

> **WORDS TO KNOW** Activity 5
>
> **claim:** (v) to say something is true
> **manage:** (v) to take care of
> **motivation:** (n) a strong reason to do something
>
> **performance:** (n) the action of doing or completing something
> **volunteer:** (v) to offer service for free

1. Opinion/Topic Sentence
2. Supporting Fact #1
3. Extra information for Supporting Fact #1
4. Supporting Fact #2

5. Extra information for Supporting Fact #2
6. Supporting Fact #3
7. Extra information for Supporting Fact #3
8. Concluding Sentence

__2__ First of all, it increases our general **motivation**.

__5__ In a recent poll by the student government, 71 percent of students who **volunteered** were better able to **manage** their time and grades.

__7__ Finally, students feel they are members of a larger community.

__4__ A large majority of students at Western High School said that they felt they were part of something greater and could see how their efforts could truly help those around them.

__3__ While some may **claim** that students should only study during the school year, research shows that volunteering improves students' motivation both in and out of the classroom.

__1__ In my opinion, all high school students should definitely volunteer in their community.

__4__ Second, volunteering helps students' academic **performance**.

__6__ Based on all of the research and results, schools should encourage students to volunteer.

Teens volunteering

Fact and Opinion

A **fact** is information that can be verified or proved. A fact is always true. In contrast, an **opinion** is what someone thinks or believes to be true. An opinion may be true or false.

FACTS	OPINIONS
Orlando is located in central Florida.	Orlando is a great city for people of all ages.
Orlando is home to several large theme parks.	There are many fun places to visit in Orlando.
The University of Central Florida is located in Orlando.	The University of Central Florida is an excellent university.
The average annual temperature is 73° F (22.78° C).	I like the weather in Orlando very much.

When you write an opinion paragraph, it is important to include facts. If you include supporting facts with examples that the reader can clearly relate to, your opinion paragraph will be stronger and you may even convince readers to agree with you.

ACTIVITY 6 | Identifying facts and opinions

Read each statement. Write *F* if it is a fact or *O* if it is an opinion.

1. __O__ Soccer is a much more interesting game to play and watch than golf.

2. __F__ In Sudan, the Nile River splits into the White Nile and the Blue Nile.

3. __O__ The most beautiful city in the world is Paris.

4. __F__ Citrus fruits include oranges, lemons, and grapefruit.

5. __O__ Hawaii is the best place for a vacation.

6. __F__ The capital of Thailand is Bangkok.

7. __F__ Security alarms are a very effective way to protect homes from burglaries.

8. __F__ School uniforms should be mandatory for all students.

9. __F__ A glass of milk has more calcium in it than a glass of apple juice.

10. __O__ Apple juice tastes better than milk.

11. __F__ Brazil is a large country in South America.

12. __O__ Everyone should take a trip to Chile.

ACTIVITY 7 | Identifying facts and opinions in a paragraph

Reread Paragraph 8.1. It contains some information that is factual and some that is the writer's opinion. Find and write two facts and two opinions.

Fact

1. _____

_____

2. _____

_____

Opinion

1. _____

_____

2. _____

_____

Topic Sentences for Opinion Paragraphs

A topic sentence for an opinion paragraph must express an opinion. If you cannot think of at least two reasons to support the opinion, it is not a good topic sentence for an opinion paragraph.

Topic Sentence:	There are several types of camels.
Problem:	This is a fact. This is an excellent topic sentence for a paragraph explaining the different kinds of camels, but it is not a good topic sentence for an opinion paragraph about camels.

Better Topic Sentence: Camels are interesting desert animals.

ACTIVITY 8 | Recognizing good topic sentences

Check (✓) the topic sentences that are good for opinion paragraphs. Be ready to explain your answers.

1. __no__ A hospital volunteer has many duties.

2. __yes__ Soccer is a much more interesting game to play and watch than golf.

3. __yes__ The largest city in Central America is Tegucigalpa, which is the capital of Honduras.

4. _Yes_ Eating a vegetarian diet is a great way to stay healthy.

5. _no_ Hawaii is the best place for a vacation.

6. _no_ The U.S. Congress has 535 members, including 100 senators.

7. _Yes_ Although Ontario is the fourth largest of the 13 provinces in Canada, it has about one-third of Canada's population and is the most populated province in the country.

8. _No_ Smartphones will completely replace laptops and tablet computers in the near future.

ACTIVITY 9 | Sequencing sentences in a paragraph

The following sentences make up a paragraph titled "Dangers of Fun in the Sun." Read the sentences and number them from 2 to 6 to indicate the correct order.

_4_ Although the damage from these rays may not be seen immediately in children, adults who spent a lot of time in the sun when they were children later have a much higher chance of developing skin cancer than those who did not.

_1_ People enjoy spending time outdoors, but too much time in the sun is dangerous and can cause serious skin damage.

_2_ According to the American Cancer Society, this disease is often a result of the sun's harmful ultraviolet rays.

_6_ In conclusion, it is very important for everyone to understand the true danger of spending too much time in the sun.

_5_ Therefore, parents should make sure that their children put on enough sunscreen before going outside.

_3_ The most serious example of this damage is skin cancer.

Grammar: Common Suffixes

Many words have different forms for different parts of speech—**noun, verb, adjective,** or **adverb**. Some words have **suffixes** (or endings) that indicate the part of speech.

PART OF SPEECH	COMMON SUFFIXES		EXAMPLES
Noun	-ion -ment -er -ness -ity -ence	vacation entertainment teacher sadness activity difference	They took a two-week **vacation** to Chile. In this photo, you can see the **difference** between a mountain and a volcano.
Verb	-ify -ize -en -ate	classify realize blacken operate	The students are **classifying** all the birds in the area. They will **operate** on the patient tomorrow.
Adjective	-ful -ent -able -ish -ial -y	beautiful different comfortable English financial windy	Are alligators and crocodiles **different**? The company has some **financial** problems.
Adverb	-ly	quickly carefully	Carlos listened **carefully** to the lecture.

Sometimes a word can function as different parts of speech. For example, the word *paint* can be a noun (*Where is the **paint**?*) or a verb (*Let's **paint** the kitchen.*). The word *hard* can be an adjective (*The candy is **hard**.*) or an adverb (*She studied **hard**.*).

ACTIVITY 10 | Identifying word forms in word families

Identify the word form(s) of each word. Write *N* (noun), *V* (verb), *ADJ* (adjective), and/or *ADV* (adverb). Some words may have more than one form (e.g., *decrease* = *N* and *V*).

1. believe _____V_____
   belief _____
   believable _____

2. finance _____
   financially _____
   financial _____

3. logically _____
   logic _____
   logical _____

4. develop _____
   developmental _____
   development _____

5. freedom _____
   freely _____
   free _____

6. increasingly _____
   increase _____
   increasing _____

7. equality _____
   equal _____
   equalize _____
   equally _____

8. simplicity _____
   simply _____
   simple _____
   simplify _____

9. legality _____
   legal _____
   legally _____
   legalize _____

ACTIVITY 11 | Correcting word forms

Each sentence has one word form error. Find the error and write the correct word form.

1. Many people did not <u>belief</u> the world was round before Christopher Columbus's voyages.

belief → believe

2. The city cannot legality build the new school on this land.

_____

3. There is going to be a new housing develop near the beach.

_____

4. On large airplanes, it is easy for passengers to stand up and walk free from one area of the plane to another.

_____

5. Though people may believe that Japanese is more difficult than English, I think the two are equal challenging.

_____

6. Babies often speak using simply words and phrases.

_____

7. At 18 years old, a child in the U.S. becomes an adult and is able to vote legal.

_____

8. Good managers can use logical to solve difficult problems.

_____

9. Unfortunately, the government's new plan may include an increasing in taxes.

_____

10. The company's finance situation has improved dramatically this year.

_____

ACTIVITY 12 | Using correct word forms

Complete the paragraph with the correct form of the word in parentheses.

> **WORDS TO KNOW** Paragraph 8.4
>
> **billion:** (n) 1,000,000,000 (also adj)
> **debt:** (n) the amount of money that you owe
> **obtain:** (v) to get or acquire through effort
>
> **occupation:** (n) a job, career
> **propose:** (v) to suggest a plan of action
> **trillion:** (n) 1,000,000,000,000 (also adj)

PARAGRAPH 8.4

Free University for All

Some people say that the United States should provide free university

1 _____ (educate), but this plan may lead to some serious problems. First, if

universities are 2 _____ (sudden) open to everyone, there will be too many

students. Even now, many universities are too 3 _____ (crowd), so where will

these new students go? Second, where will the money come from? University education is

not free. It will cost the government a lot. Can the government 4 _____ (add)

billions more to the **trillion**-dollar **debt** it already has? Society needs electricians, plumbers,

truck 5 _____ (drive), and cashiers, and a university education is not a

6 _____ (require) for these **occupations**. Finally, if so many people **obtain** a

university degree, then the value of that degree will decrease, which will reduce people's job

possibilities. Although the idea of free university education 7 _____ (certain)

sounds like a good idea and a 8 _____ (major) of people may think it is a

great idea, this 9 _____ (**propose**) has several problems that people are not

considering. Therefore, providing a free university education to everyone is not a good

10 _____ (solve).

Developing Ideas for an Opinion Paragraph

One good source for topics for opinion paragraphs is the news. Top stories and editorial articles may give you some ideas.

Two methods of brainstorming work well for opinion paragraphs. One method is to brainstorm using clusters as you did in Unit 2. A second method is to create a chart. Write the topic and make two columns underneath. In one column list the negative ideas; in the other, list the positive ideas.

Here is an example of a negative-positive brainstorm chart.

TOPIC: FREE COLLEGE OR UNIVERSITY CLASSES	
NEGATIVE	POSITIVE
1. costs a lot of money 2. not everyone wants or needs	1. raises the education level of all people 2. creates more jobs

After listing all the negative and positive points, you can decide which points will be the most useful for your paragraph.

ACTIVITY 13 | Brainstorming for an opinion paragraph

Should people use less plastic? Brainstorm negative and positive aspects of using plastic. Discuss your charts with a partner.

TOPIC: USING PLASTIC	
NEGATIVE	POSITIVE
1.	1.
2.	2.
3.	3.

ACTIVITY 14 | Writing a topic sentence

Write a topic sentence for the topic in Activity 13.

_____

_____

BUILDING BETTER VOCABULARY

WORDS TO KNOW

ban (n)	freedom (n)	old-fashioned (adj)
benefit (n) AW	injure (v) AW	performance (n)
billion (n & adj)	interact (v) AW	prohibit (v) AW
claim (v)	manage (v)	propose (v)
common sense (n)	mandatory (adj)	trillion (n & adj)
concentrate (v) AW	motivation (n) AW	versus (prep)
damage (n)	obtain (v) AW	volunteer (v) AW
debt (n)	occupation (n) AW	waste time (phr)

ACTIVITY 15 | Word associations

Circle the word or phrase that is more closely related to the bold word on the left.

1. ban	allow	not allow
2. claim	ask	say
3. debt	owe	wish
4. injure	help	hurt
5. mandatory	must	might
6. obtain	get	not get
7. occupation	job	owner
8. prohibit	permit	not permit
9. propose	suggest	wonder
10. volunteer	paid	unpaid

ACTIVITY 16 | Collocations

Fill in the blank with the word that most naturally completes the phrase.

benefits	common	interact	old-fashioned	waste

1. a _____ of time

2. an _____ idea

3. _____ sense

4. _____ of a healthy diet

5. _____ with someone

claim	damage	occupations	prohibit	versus

6. _____ that something is true

7. _____ the sale of cigarettes to teenagers

8. _____ from a strong storm

9. _____ with high salaries

10. one team _____ another

ACTIVITY 17 | Word forms

Complete each sentence with the correct word form. Use the correct forms of the words.

NOUN	VERB	ADJECTIVE	SENTENCES
benefit	benefit	beneficial	**1.** Exercising two or three times a week can be _____ to your health. **2.** Some scientists say listening to music can _____ someone who is lonely.
concentration	concentrate	concentrated	**3.** Music helps some people _____ . **4.** This job will require a lot of _____ .
damage	damage	damaged damaging	**5.** The weather report says that the area may experience _____ winds tonight. **6.** How much _____ did the storm do?
occupation	occupy	occupied	**7.** How do you _____ your time when you are on vacation? **8.** Excuse me, is this seat _____ ?
proposal	propose		**9.** A good manager will _____ multiple plans. **10.** Which is the best _____ ?

ACTIVITY 18 | Vocabulary in writing

Choose five words from Words to Know. Write a complete sentence with each word. Write three facts and two opinions.

1. _____

_____

2. _____

_____

3. _____

_____

4. _____

_____

5. _____

_____

BUILDING BETTER SENTENCES

ACTIVITY 19 | Editing

Each sentence has (x) number of errors. Find and correct them.

1. If a majority voters vote in favor of the new plan, taxes will to increase. (2)

2. A study recent showed that people in big cities voted very different than people in rural areas. (2)

3. Although biking is very popular, but many people prefer walking as their most common mode in transportation. (2)

4. Pilots will not landing in very bad weather, because they do not want endanger the passengers. (3)

5. One of the main reason for the increasing number of car accidents are an increase in the number of people driving when they sleepy. (3)

ACTIVITY 20 | Word prompts for sentence writing

Write an original sentence using the words and/or phrases. Use correct punctuation.

1. (Although /other students) _____

_____

2. (Because / many travelers) _____

_____

3. (While / may think) _____

_____

4. (A majority of / but) _____

_____

5. (One / most important reasons) _____

_____

ACTIVITY 21 | Combining sentences

Combine the ideas into one sentence. You may change the word forms, but do not change or omit any ideas. There may be more than one answer.

1. Teachers require their best students to read articles.
These articles are from journals.
These are additional articles.
The teachers teach history.
This action may happen.
Some teachers do this.

_____

_____

2. A tomato is a vegetable.
Many people believe this.
A tomato is actually a fruit.
Several facts show this.

_____

_____

3. People should not throw stones.
These people live in houses.
The houses are made of glass.
A proverb says this.
This is a well-known proverb.

_____

_____

WRITING

ACTIVITY 22 | Writing a paragraph

Write a paragraph about a strong opinion that you have. Follow these guidelines.

1. Choose a topic from the unit that you disagree with, or give your opinion about one of these topics:
   - Is living abroad beneficial?
   - Do young children need their own cell phones?

2. Brainstorm your topic. If you want, use the Internet for ideas.

3. Use the chart below to list negative and positive points about your topic.

4. Write a topic sentence with a controlling idea.

5. Write supporting sentences with facts that support your opinions.

6. Check for incorrect word forms.

7. Use at least two of the vocabulary words or phrases presented in Words to Know. Underline these words and phrases in your paragraph.

TOPIC:	
NEGATIVE POINTS	POSITIVE POINTS

ACTIVITY 23 | Peer editing

Work with a partner. Read your partner's paragraph from Activity 22. Use Peer Editing Form 8 in the *Writer's Handbook*. Offer positive suggestions to help your partner write a better paragraph. Consider your partner's comments as you revise your paragraph.

Additional Topics for Writing

Here are more ideas for opinion paragraphs. When you write, follow the guidelines in Activity 22.

TOPIC 1: Look at the photo at the beginning of the unit and at the ideas and topic sentence you wrote in Activities 13 and 14. Do you think single-use plastic (straws, bags, food containers) should be banned? Why or why not?

TOPIC 2: Do you think professional athletes receive too much money? Why or why not?

TOPIC 3: Should students have to take an entrance exam to enter a college or university? Why or why not?

TOPIC 4: Should schools last all year (12 months)? Why or why not?

TOPIC 5: Is working and studying at the same time good for students? Why or why not?

TEST PREP

> **TIP**
>
> Do not use contractions. In academic writing, you should stay away from informal language. Write out your contractions (You're = You are; I'm = I am) to make the writing sound more formal and academic.

You should spend about 25 minutes on this task. Write a paragraph with 6–10 sentences.

In many places, the age necessary to obtain a driver's license is 16 or 17. Many people say this age should be increased to 21. In your opinion, what should the required age be to get a driver's license?

Be sure to include a topic sentence, supporting sentences, and a concluding sentence. Write at least 150 words.

9 | Narrative Paragraphs

OBJECTIVES
- Analyze a narrative paragraph
- Use the simple past and past progressive in time clauses
- Use adjectives for more descriptive language
- Write a narrative paragraph

A team competes in a flying machine competition. Participants try to fly homemade flying machines that they make. Most competitors enter the competition for fun and their machines do not usually fly very well.

FREEWRITE | Look at the photo. What are these people doing? What do you think happened before this photo? After? Imagine and describe the events of this team's day.

ELEMENTS OF GREAT WRITING

What Is a Narrative Paragraph?

A **narrative paragraph** tells a story or describes an event. For example, when you watch a movie, you are usually watching a narrative. A narrative paragraph can be fun to write because you often describe an event from your life.

A narrative paragraph:

- tells a story
- has a clear beginning, a middle, and an end
- uses descriptive words to help the reader better understand exact feelings and events

In an academic setting, a narrative paragraph is sometimes used in reports. For example, you may need to observe or record events, such as when conducting an experiment in a science class. Creative writing or theater classes may also involve narrative writing.

ACTIVITY 1 | Ordering a story

Look at the photo. How does the speaker feel? Tell a partner. Then read the parts of the paragraph and put them in the correct order (2–5).

> **WORDS TO KNOW** Activity 1
>
> **get over:** (phr v) to recover from
> **realize:** (v) to understand; to start to believe something is true
>
> **take a deep breath:** (phr) to relax for a moment
> **task:** (n) a job or assignment
> **strategy:** (n) a plan to achieve a goal

a. ___3___ I followed all of the **strategies** that my teacher gave us. I wrote all of my ideas on note cards. I practiced my speech with my notes in front of a mirror, in front of my cat, and in front of a friend. Would I be able to make my speech in front of my whole class?

b. ___4___ When the day of my speech came, I was ready. As I reached the front of the class, I looked at my classmates and smiled. Then I looked down at my note cards. At that moment, I **realized** that I had the wrong information. These were the notes for my biology test, not the information about my speech! I closed my eyes and **took a deep breath**.

c. ___1___ I never thought I could do it, but I finally **got over** my fear of public speaking.

d. ___5___ Then I began my speech. To my surprise, I spoke without stopping. Three minutes later, it was over. Everyone loved it, and I felt like a winner.

e. ___2___ At the beginning of the semester, my English teacher assigned us the difficult **task** of speaking in front of the class for three minutes, and I worried about it for the next two months.

Parts of a Narrative Paragraph

Topic Sentence

The first sentence in a narrative paragraph—the topic sentence—explains the main idea of the story that will follow. It prepares readers for the action that will come.

Beginning of the Story

The beginning of the story, or the start of the action, comes after the topic sentence. It "sets the scene" for the story. It helps readers understand where the story takes place and any feelings people have.

Middle of the Story

The middle part is where the main action or problem occurs.

End of the Story

The end of the story gives the final action or result. If there is a problem or conflict in the story, the solution is presented here.

ACTIVITY 2 | Noticing the parts of the narrative paragraph

Reread the story in Activity 1 in the correct order. Match the letters (b-e) to the four parts of the paragraph.

Topic Sentence: _____   Middle of the Story: ___a___, ___b___

Beginning of the Story: _____   End of the Story: ___d___

ACTIVITY 3 | Analyzing a narrative paragraph

Read the narrative paragraph and answer the questions that follow.

> **WORDS TO KNOW** Paragraph 9.1
>
> **come up to:** (v phr) to approach, get near
> **incredibly:** (adv) very, extremely
>
> **remind:** (v) to cause a person to remember

PARAGRAPH 9.1

My Department Store Nightmare

I will never forget the first time I got lost in New York City. — Topic Sentence

I was traveling with my parents during winter vacation. We were in an incredibly large department store, and I was so excited to see such a huge place. — Beginning (background)

Suddenly, I turned around to ask my mom something, but she was gone! I began crying loudly. A salesclerk **came up to** me and asked if I was OK. She told the store management that a little boy with blue jeans and a red cap was lost. Two minutes later, my mom and dad came running toward me. We all cried and hugged each other. — Middle (action)

This story took place more than 20 years ago, but every time I see a department store, it reminds me of that scared little boy. — End (result)

1. What is the purpose of this paragraph? _____

_____

2. Where does the story take place? _____

3. Reread the middle of the story. Put the events in order.

   a. __4__ The salesclerk talked to store management.

   b. __3__ The salesclerk talked to the boy.

   c. __2__ The boy started crying.

   d. __1__ The boy got separated from his mother.

4. How does this story end? _____

_____

ACTIVITY 4 | Analyzing narrative paragraphs

Read the titles of Paragraphs 9.2 and 9.3. Tell a partner what you think each paragraph is about. Then read the paragraphs and answer the questions that follow each one.

> **WORDS TO KNOW** Paragraphs 9.2 to 9.3
>
> **capture:** (v) to catch
> **casually:** (adv) in a relaxed manner
> **funny:** (adj) causing laughter; odd
> **instant:** (n) a very quick period of time; less than a second
>
> **painful:** (adj) causing pain; hurting
> **relationship:** (n) connection between two people or things
> **unexpected:** (adj) surprising
> **valuable:** (adj) having worth or value

PARAGRAPH 9.2

The Photo That Changed His Life

It was a freezing cold winter day, and mountain climber Cory Richards was climbing down from Gasherbrum II, the 13th-tallest mountain peak in the world, when his life changed in an **instant**. The mountain, which lies between Pakistan and China, is not an easy one to climb and the cold that day was **painful**. As Richards and his team were climbing down, they heard a noise and looked up. They saw a wall of snow and ice coming toward them. They were all hit and thrown to the ground. Luckily all of them lived to tell about it. After he saw that his partners were safe, Richards took photos of himself, which **captured** the terror he had just experienced. One of these photos was on the cover of *National Geographic Magazine*. Soon he was a well-known photographer and explorer for National Geographic. Sometimes something **unexpected** can change your life forever.

1. What is the purpose of this paragraph? _____

_____

2. What background is given in the paragraph? _____

_____

3. What is the main action in the middle of the story? _____

_____

4. How does the story end? _____

_____

A Lesson in Friendship

I learned the hard way how to make friends in a new school. At my old school in Toronto, I was on the football and track teams, so I was very popular and had a lot of friends. Everything changed when I was 16 years old because my parents decided to move to Florida. Going to a new school was not easy for me. The first few days in my new school were extremely difficult. The class schedule was different, and the teachers were more informal than in my old school. All the students dressed **casually** in shorts and t-shirts instead of a school uniform. Some kids tried to be nice to me, but I did not want to talk to them. To me, they looked and acted **funny**! After a few weeks, I realized that no one even tried to talk to me anymore. I began to feel lonely. Two months passed before I got the courage to talk to a few classmates. Finally, I realized that they were normal people, just like me. I began to develop some **relationships**, many of which are now good friendships. I learned a **valuable** lesson[1] about making friends that year.

[1]learn a lesson: to learn correct behavior from a bad experience

1. What is the purpose of this paragraph?

_____

_____

2. What is the background information in this paragraph? Why is it important?

_____

_____

3. What lesson did the writer learn from this experience? Write a final sentence for the paragraph stating the lesson the writer learned. Begin with *I learned that* . . .

_____

_____

ACTIVITY 5 | Recognizing good topics for narrative paragraphs

Check (✓) the titles that you think would make good narrative paragraphs. Discuss your choices with a partner. Explain your reasons.

❏ Luke's Adventure in Nepal   ❏ Natural Disasters

❏ How to Become a Doctor   ❏ Lions: Kings of the Jungle

❏ The Graduation Party   ❏ A Great Day in the Mountains

ACTIVITY 6 | Brainstorming for a narrative paragraph

Think about a special day in your life. On a separate piece of paper, list at least five things that happened that day.

Using Descriptive Language to Improve a Narrative

In narrative writing, you want the readers to be able to imagine that they are actually in the story. In order to do this, you should describe the story and experiences as carefully as possible. Use exact, or *precise*, vocabulary to help your readers imagine and feel the emotions of the story.

GENERAL DESCRIPTION	MORE PRECISE ADJECTIVES
The book was <u>nice</u>.	interesting, thrilling, inspiring, heartwarming, superb
These TV shows are <u>bad</u>.	boring, horrible, empty, dull, shocking, violent
The swimmer felt <u>great</u>.	marvelous, fantastic, elated, wonderful, relaxed
We were <u>afraid</u>.	terrified, anxious, alarmed, scared, petrified

ACTIVITY 7 | Describing a moment

Look at the photograph. What do you think happened before this moment? What do you think happened right after? Discuss your ideas in a group.

A person stands in a tree above an angry-looking grizzly bear.

ACTIVITY 8 | Writing about a moment

Write about the photo you discussed in Activity 7. Imagine the story. Complete the frame with your ideas, using more precise words. Use a dictionary to help you.

Moment: _____

Where was this? _____

What happened?

Before: _____

_____

During: _____

_____

After: _____

_____

What was the person in the photo feeling?

Before: _____

_____

During: _____

_____

After: _____

_____

Did the person in the photo learn something? _____

_____

Grammar: Simple Past and Past Progressive

When writers tell a story, they usually use the simple past or the past progressive. The simple past is more common. Time clauses help to clarify when the event happened.

EXPLANATION	EXAMPLES
Use the **simple past** to show that something happened in the past.	I **visited** Mexico in 2017.
Use the **past progressive** to show that something was in progress at a specific past time.	At that time, my friends **were living** in Mexico.
Use a time clause with a time word (*when, before, after, while*) to specify when an event in the main clause happened.	**While I was in Mexico**, I **lost** my passport. My friends **were driving** through town **when the earthquake happened.**

ACTIVITY 9 | Choosing correct verb forms

Write the simple past or past progressive form of the verbs.

> **WORDS TO KNOW** Paragraph 9.4
>
> **document:** (n) an official paper or form
> **frighten:** (v) to make a person afraid
> **shocked:** (adj) surprised in a bad way
>
> **silence:** (n) lack of sound
> **valid:** (adj) legally usable for a set time period
> **wonder:** (v) to think about

PARAGRAPH 9.4

Ali's Surprise

Ali [1] _____ (know) it was difficult to get a student visa, so he [2] _____ (follow) all of the instructions. First, he collected all the necessary paperwork, including his I–20 **document**, passport, and bank statements. On the morning of his interview, he [3] _____ (get) on a bus to the capital. For five long hours, while he [4] _____ (ride) in **silence**, he [5] _____ (look) out of the window and **wondered** about his day. When he [6] _____ (arrive) at the embassy, he [7] _____ (see) a line of more than 100 people. He patiently waited. The faces of the embassy workers **frightened** him, except for an older woman who reminded him of his grandmother. She [8] _____ (work) at window number 4. He hoped that she would be the one to look at his paperwork. When it was his turn, he looked up quickly. A baby-faced worker at window number 3 [9] _____ (call) him to come up. Ali [10] _____ (go) to the young embassy employee's window. He looked sadly over at "Grandma." Then he [11] _____ (hear) her exclaim to the person at her window, "You will never get a visa! Next in line, please." Ali was **shocked**. He [12] _____ (turn) to the worker in front of him, and the worker [13] _____ (say), "Here you are, sir. Your student visa is **valid** for one year." Ali could not believe it. As he [14] _____ (leave), he [15] _____ (take) a selfie and [16] _____ (send) it to his family with the news. Soon he would be a student in the United States.

ACTIVTY 10 | Editing the simple past and past progressive

Read the paragraph. Find and correct the eleven errors with the simple past or past progressive.

WORDS TO KNOW Paragraph 9.5

advertising: (n) the field of creating descriptions (for TV, radio, …) to promote products

communication: (n) giving and receiving information by speech, writing, or signs

---

PARAGRAPH 9.5

My First Job

The happiest day of my life is when I get my first job last year. After college, I try for six months to get a job with an **advertising** firm, but my luck is bad. Finally, one day my life changed. While I am eating a sandwich in a downtown coffee shop, my luck began to change. A young woman who was sitting next to me asks if she could read my newspaper. I said OK, and we start talking. She begins to tell me about herself. She was an executive in a huge advertising company and is looking for an assistant. I told her that I was very interested in mass **communication**. She gives me her business card, and within one week, I get a job as her assistant. It was the best lunch of my life!

BUILDING BETTER VOCABULARY

WORDS TO KNOW

advertising (n)	get over (phr v)	silence (n)
capture (v)	incredibly (adv) AW	strategy (n) AW
casually (adv)	instant (n)	take a deep breath (phr)
come up to (v phr)	painful (adj) AW	task (n) AW
communication (n) AW	realize (v)	unexpected (adj)
document (n) AW	relationship: (n)	valid (adj) AW
frighten (v)	remind (v)	valuable (adj)
funny (adj)	shocked (adj)	wonder (v)

ACTIVITY 11 | Word associations

Circle the word or phrase that is more closely related to the bold word on the left.

1. casually	serious	relaxed
2. document	paper	plastic
3. frighten	afraid	surprised
4. get over	accept a gift	be OK again
5. incredibly	easy to believe	hard to believe
6. shocked	afraid	surprised
7. silence	no money	no sound
8. strategy	plan	do not plan
9. task	play	job
10. valuable	cheap	expensive

ACTIVITY 12 | Collocations

Fill in the blank with the word that most naturally completes the phrase.

capture	frightened	instant	realized	reply

1. _____ to an email

2. happened in an _____

3. _____ that I made a mistake

4. to _____ a special moment

5. _____ by a loud noise

advertising	relationship	reminds	valid	wonder

6. _____ me of my childhood

7. an _____ strategy

8. a _____ passport

9. a good _____ with your family

10. _____ why something happened

ACTIVITY 13 | Word forms

Complete each sentence with the correct word form. Use the correct forms of the words.

NOUN	VERB	ADJECTIVE	ADVERB	SENTENCES
advertisement advertising	advertise	advertising		1. She got a job at an _____ agency. 2. We need to _____ online.
fright	frighten	frightened frightening		3. Sleeping in a dark room might _____ some children. 4. The cats were _____ when they heard the thunder.
		incredible	incredibly	5. His speech was _____. 6. I was _____ happy when my presentation was over.
pain		painful	painfully	7. The _____ is in his lower back. 8. The surgery was _____, but the patient recovered quickly.
silence	silence	silent	silently	9. They _____ took the test. 10. They worked in complete _____.

ACTIVITY 14 | Vocabulary in writing

Choose five words from Words to Know. Write a complete sentence with each word.

1. _____

_____

2. _____

_____

3. _____

_____

4. _____

_____

5. _____

_____

BUILDING BETTER SENTENCES

ACTIVITY 15 | Editing

Each sentence has (x) number of errors. Find and correct them.

1. On March 27, 1964, Alaska had severe earthquake that cause 139 deaths. (2)

2. The first of the famous *Star Wars* movie was released to the public in May 25, 1977. (2)

3. When it was time for board my flight for Tokyo, I could no find my boarding pass. (2)

4. The airport in San Francisco often experience long flight delays because fog. (2)

5. Alaska becomes a state on 1959. (2)

ACTIVITY 16 | Scrambled sentences

Unscramble the words and phrases to write complete sentences. More than one answer may be possible.

1. I did not have my / as soon as / realized that / the hotel, I / laptop with me / I arrived at

   _____

   _____

2. years old / day of my life / occurred when I / the worst / was 31

   _____

   _____

3. day of the / on the second / go to the hospital / had a car / accident and had to / trip, Matt

   _____

   _____

4. the new vocabulary / first, I / that I did not / wrote down all / know yet

   _____

   _____

5. my most embarrassing / about 15 years old / a supermarket when / moment took / I was / place at

   _____

   _____

ACTIVITY 17 | Combining sentences

Combine the ideas into one sentence. You may change the word forms, but do not change or omit any ideas. There may be more than one correct answer.

1. She was born in central Florida.
   She was born in a town.
   The town was small.
   This happened in 2000.
   This happened on January 18.

   _____

   _____

2. My graduation was the most important day.
   I graduated from high school.
   This was the most important day in my life.
   This is certainly true.

   _____

   _____

3. I was sitting on a train.
   My best friend was sitting on the same train.
   The train was in Frankfurt.
   The train was going to Paris.
   This is when our nightmare began.
   Our nightmare was long.

   _____

   _____

WRITING

ACTIVITY 18 | Writing a paragraph

Write a narrative paragraph about an experience that you have had. Follow these guidelines.

1. Choose a special event in your life to write about, such as your graduation day or the first time you did something.

2. Brainstorm the events in your story.

3. Write a topic sentence with a controlling idea.

4. Give enough background information to help your readers understand the setting.

5. Write supporting sentences for the middle of your narrative.

6. Use descriptive words.

7. Write the end of the story.

8. Use at least two of the vocabulary words or phrases presented in Words to Know. Underline these words and phrases in your paragraph.

9. Check for accuracy of simple past and past progressive verbs.

ACTIVITY 19 | Peer editing

Work with a partner. Read your partner's paragraph from Activity 18. Then use Peer Editing Form 9 in the *Writer's Handbook*. Offer positive suggestions to help your partner write a better paragraph. Consider your partner's comments as you revise your paragraph.

Additional Topics for Writing

Here are more ideas for narrative paragraphs. When you write your paragraph, follow the guidelines in Activity 18.

TOPIC 1:   Look at the photo at the beginning of this unit. Imagine and tell a story describing how they came to be in this situation.

TOPIC 2:   Tell a story from your own country or culture that you think foreigners would not know.

TOPIC 3:   Write about how someone you know got in trouble. What happened?

TOPIC 4:   Write about an important lesson that you learned from a real experience.

TOPIC 5:   Write about the most memorable movie you have seen. Briefly explain the plot (story) of the film.

TEST PREP

TIP

Avoid using general or vague vocabulary. Words such as *nice*, *good*, and *very* can often be changed to more specific terms, such as *friendly*, *fabulous*, and *incredibly*. Be more precise in your word choice.

You should spend about 25 minutes on this task. Write a paragraph with 6–10 sentences.

What is a time when you or someone you know got caught doing something wrong? Tell what you did, what was happening when you were caught, and what happened afterward.

Use past time clauses with the simple past and past progressive. Write at least 150 words.

10 | From Paragraphs to Essays

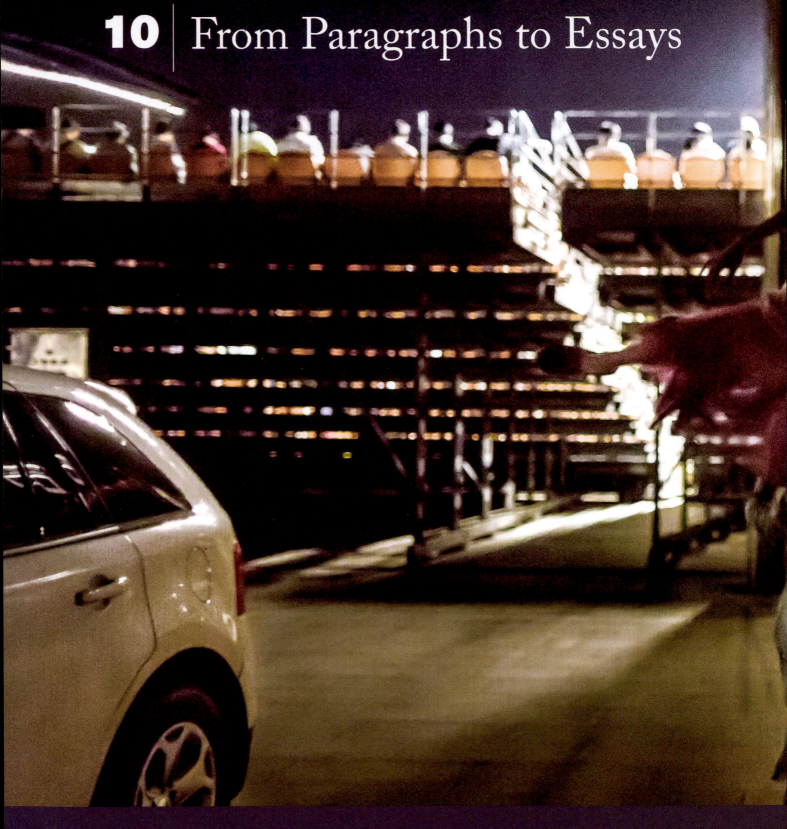

OBJECTIVES
- Analyze an essay
- Outline an essay
- Learn about introduction paragraphs and thesis statements
- Learn about body and concluding paragraphs
- Write an essay

A couple dances backstage at an outdoor theater in a car park in Hangzhou, China.

ELEMENTS OF GREAT WRITING

What Is an Essay?

An **essay** is a collection of paragraphs that presents facts, opinions, and ideas on a topic. Essays are written for many different purposes: to explain, to argue, to describe, to show cause and effect, to tell a story, etc. Essays differ in length. They can be as short as one page with three paragraphs or as long as ten or more pages with many paragraphs.

Students write essays in many academic areas, such as English composition, science, and history. Essays are also required on standardized tests such as SAT®, TOEFL®, and IELTS®.

Essays are similar in structure to paragraphs, but they include more information.

How are Essays and Paragraphs Related?

Notice how paragraphs and essays have a similar structure. Both start with the main idea (topic sentence or thesis statement), include supporting information, and end with concluding comments.

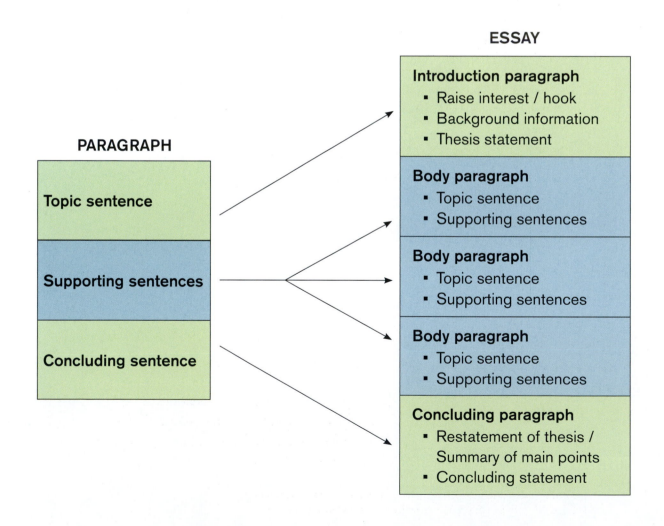

PARAGRAPH

- Topic sentence
- Supporting sentences
- Concluding sentence

ESSAY

Introduction paragraph
- Raise interest / hook
- Background information
- Thesis statement

Body paragraph
- Topic sentence
- Supporting sentences

Body paragraph
- Topic sentence
- Supporting sentences

Body paragraph
- Topic sentence
- Supporting sentences

Concluding paragraph
- Restatement of thesis / Summary of main points
- Concluding statement

ACTIVITY 1 | Analyzing an essay

Read the essay. The thesis statement is underlined in paragraph 1. Underline the topic sentence in each body paragraph. Then answer the questions that follow.

WORDS TO KNOW Essay 10.1

accomplish: (v) to succeed in doing
deadly: (adj) causing a person to die
decade: (n) a period of 10 years
discovery: (n) the finding of something new
focus: (v) to center one's attention on

invention: (n) something useful created by someone
prevent: (v) to stop from happening
technology: (n) the use of science to create practical or useful things

---

ESSAY 10.1

The Most Important Discovery of the Last Century

1   If you ask someone about the most important **discovery** or **invention** in the last hundred years, you will hear many different answers. Some people might answer with some form of **technology,** such as the video camera, the cell phone, or the Internet, because they have changed our lives in big ways. <u>However, in my opinion, antibiotics[1] are the most important discovery because they have allowed people to live longer.</u>

Introduction (with thesis)

2   In the past, people did not live as long because they often died from bacterial infections,[2] but this is not true today. Even as recently as 100 years ago, bacterial infections were **deadly**. Something as small as a simple cut on a finger could cause the person to die. The world changed, however, in 1928 when penicillin was discovered. This new drug **prevented** many common infections from getting worse. It was the first antibiotic, and since its discovery, people have been able to live longer.

3   Because of antibiotics, people suddenly had longer lives and, therefore, time to **accomplish** more things. In 1850, people lived to an average age of 38, but in 1950, people lived to an average age of 58. This increase meant more time for people to **focus** on becoming presidents, doctors, or inventors. In particular, penicillin was a very important discovery because people's average life expectancy increased greatly in the **decade** (1920–30) when it was discovered.

Body

4   While technology has been important, the discovery of antibiotics has meant more to people than anything else. People live longer and can, therefore, accomplish more. If there were no antibiotics, we would not be able to enjoy the quality of life that we have today.

Conclusion

[1]antibiotic: a medicine that slows down or stops the spread of infection
[2]bacterial infection: an infection caused by germs (tiny living things)

1. Read the thesis statement in Essay 10.1, paragraph 1, and the topic sentences in paragraphs 2 and 3. Explain to a partner how the two topic sentences relate to the thesis.

2. In the introduction, how does the writer get the reader interested?

   _____

3. Read the introduction and the conclusion. How are they related?

   _____

   _____

An Essay Outline

Before you write an essay, an important step is to make an outline. An **outline** will help you to organize your ideas and stay focused as you write. Each number in an outline represents a paragraph in an essay. Here is an outline for an essay with five paragraphs, but the number of paragraphs can vary from three to more than ten.

I. Introduction	It explains the purpose of the essay and states a thesis (the main idea of the essay).
II. Body **III.** Body **IV.** Body	Each has a topic sentence with a main idea that supports the thesis; each topic sentence is developed with supporting sentences.
V. Conclusion	It restates the thesis or main idea of the essay and summarizes or finishes the essay in a clear way.

ACTIVITY 2 | Outlining an essay

Complete the outline of Essay 10.1. Write information about each paragraph in the essay.

I. Introduction (What is the thesis statement?) _However, in my opinion, antibiotics are_

   the most important discovery because they have allowed people to live longer.

II. Body _____

   _____

III. Body _____

   _____

IV. Conclusion (What does it do?) _____

   _____

The Introduction Paragraph

The **introduction paragraph** is the first paragraph of an essay. It is an important part of the essay because it tells the reader what the essay will discuss. In addition, the introduction should be interesting so that people will want to read the essay. It should also give background information and show how the essay is organized.

The Thesis Statement

Just as the most important part of any paragraph is the topic sentence, the most important part of an introduction to an essay is the **thesis statement**. A thesis statement tells the reader what the essay is about and the writer's overall idea of the topic. The thesis statement may also indicate what the organization of the essay will be. The thesis statement is often near the end of the introduction paragraph. A strong thesis statement provides an idea that can be supported with several points.

Here are two examples of strong thesis statements:

Reading helps children to increase their vocabulary, become independent thinkers, and experience a different world through stories.

Shakespeare's Romeo and Juliet *is an outstanding story because it makes us question whether we are more important than our family.*

ACTIVITY 3 | Analyzing the introduction paragraph

Read the first paragraph of Essay 10.1 again. Answer the questions.

1. How many sentences are there before the thesis statement? _____

2. What is the purpose of the sentences before the thesis statement? _____

_____

ACTIVITY 4 | Identifying good thesis statements

Check (✓) the two best thesis statements. Be prepared to explain your answers.

1. _____ Three things make traveling to Southeast Asia an unforgettable experience.

2. _____ Buenos Aires is the capital of Argentina, which is the second-largest country in South America.

3. _____ All high school students should be required to take a course in cooking.

4. _____ People often make mistakes when trying to spell verbs like *receive* and *believe* because they confuse *ei* with *ie*.

5. _____ My aunt Josephine was born in 1951.

6. _____ Plastic is used for many food products.

Body Paragraphs

Essays need supporting points just like paragraphs do. There should be at least two or three ideas that support the thesis statement. Each of these ideas will eventually become a separate **body paragraph**.

Asking a question about the thesis statement is a good way to come up with material for supporting paragraphs.

Thesis Statement: Three things make traveling to Southeast Asia an unforgettable experience.

Question: Why is it an unforgettable experience?

Possible ideas to develop:

- friendly people
- beautiful places to see
- delicious food

The essay outline might look like this.

I.   **Introduction** with thesis: Three things make traveling to Southeast Asia an unforgettable experience.

II. **Body:** friendly people

III. **Body:** beautiful places to see

IV. **Body:** delicious food

V.   **Conclusion**

ACTIVITY 5 | Planning body paragraphs from a thesis statement

Study the thesis statement. Then write a question and possible ideas for the body paragraphs.

Thesis Statement: All high school students should be required to take a course in cooking.

Question:

_____

Possible ideas to develop:

_____

_____

_____

_____

_____

_____

The Concluding Paragraph

The last paragraph in an essay is the **concluding paragraph**. The concluding paragraph sometimes offers a suggestion, gives an opinion, or makes a prediction about the future. It can also just restate or briefly summarize information in the essay. The concluding paragraph should not contain any new information.

ACTIVITY 6 | Purpose of a concluding paragraph

Read the introduction and concluding paragraph from Essay 10.1. List some topics that are similar between the two paragraphs.

_____

_____

_____

ACTIVITY 7 | Writing an original concluding paragraph

Work with a partner to write a simple concluding paragraph for an essay on a required cooking class for high school students. Look back at the thesis statement and ideas you wrote in Activity 5 to help you.

_____

_____

_____

_____

_____

_____

_____

ACTIVITY 8 | Analyzing an essay

Read the essay. Then choose the best answer to each question that follows.

> **WORDS TO KNOW** Essay 10.2
>
> **basic:** (adj) major; essential
> **bilingual:** (adj) able to speak two languages
> **expression:** (n) a group of words; an idiom
>
> **frequently:** (adv) often
> **maintain:** (v) to keep at the same level

The Benefits of Being Bilingual

1   The Vieira family moved from Brazil to the United States in 2001. At that time, they made a decision. They decided to stop speaking Portuguese at home and only communicate in English. They were, in fact, living in an English-speaking country. The Vieira children are adults now, and from time to time they travel to Brazil to visit family and old friends. There is a problem, however. Mr. and Mrs. Vieira's children cannot communicate with their relatives. This same situation happens **frequently** all over the world. When people move to a new country, many of them begin to forget not only their culture but also their first language, and as time passes, they lose the many benefits of being **bilingual**.

2   One of the most **basic** advantages of being bilingual is easier communication with more people around the world. People who can speak both English and Spanish, for example, can travel to more countries without worrying about communication. In contrast, people who are monolingual must depend on others in order to communicate. Using another person to translate for you is not the same as being able to understand speakers yourself. Because bilingual speakers are in complete control of their own words and ideas, communication is more direct and easier.

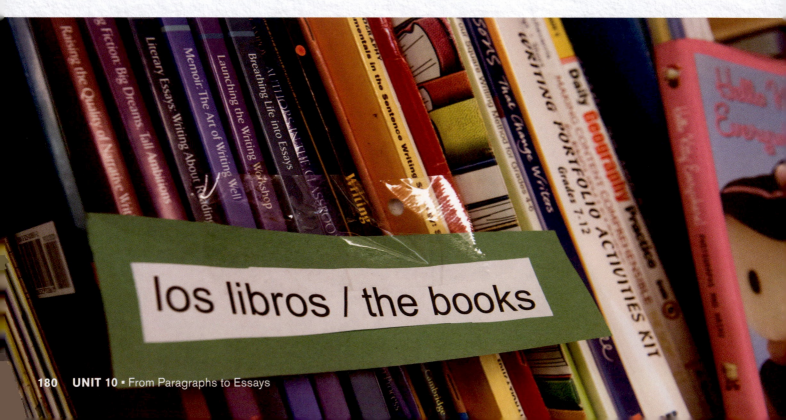

los libros / the books

3   Speaking a second language also allows people to learn about another culture through the special words and phrases in that language. For example, a person who speaks North American English knows the **expression** "meat and potatoes." If we say someone is a meat and potatoes kind of person, it means that person does not like special food. Therefore, it also tells us that in this culture, meat and potatoes—not rice, not pasta, not fish—are considered normal food. In English, *to rat on someone* is to tell someone else what that person did, and *to be a rat* is to be a bad person. From these expressions, we can tell that a rat is a bad animal in this culture, but a rat may be good in another culture. Finally, through the baseball expressions *to hit a home run* (to do something that is very successful) or *to strike out* (to fail completely), we learn that the sport of baseball is important in North American culture. Thus, becoming bilingual can increase knowledge of not only a new language but also a new culture.

4   Finally, bilingualism can help people from different countries, languages, and cultures get along better. If everyone in the world spoke a second or third language, it would be much easier to understand other people's ideas, beliefs, and actions. This would also include a better understanding of the problems and situations in other countries. If we can understand each other more, perhaps we can accept our differences and get along better.

5   The benefits of bilingualism are clear. Being bilingual helps with communicating, learning a new culture, and getting along with other people. People who already have the gift of speaking another language sometimes forget it and lose the ability to communicate in their first language. If they do not try to **maintain** their first language, they will clearly miss out on all the wonderful benefits of being bilingual.

1. How does the essay begin?

   a. with a story   **b.** with an opinion   **c.** with a fact

2. Reread the concluding paragraph. Which word best describes it?

   a. a suggestion   **b.** an opinion   **c.** a prediction

3. Which paragraph gives a specific example of a cultural phrase to support the idea of the benefits of bilingualism?

   a. Paragraph 2   **b.** Paragraph 3   **c.** Paragraph 4

4. Which paragraph discusses the benefits of bilingualism for international relations?

   a. Paragraph 2   **b.** Paragraph 3   **c.** Paragraph 4

5. Which paragraph talks about a specific disadvantage of speaking only one language?

   a. Paragraph 2   **b.** Paragraph 3   **c.** Paragraph 5

Different Kinds of Essay Organization

Once you write a thesis statement, you are ready to organize the ideas for your essay. Here are two examples of essay outlines.

Opinion Essay Outline

Thesis Statement: Traveling to Southeast Asia is an unforgettable experience.

  I. Introduction

II. Body: Friendly people

III. Body: Beautiful sights

IV. Body: Delicious food

  V. Conclusion

Process Essay Outline

Thesis Statement: There are several steps a student should take to get into an American university.

  I. Introduction

II. Body: Learn English

III. Body: Prepare for and take the TOEFL®

IV. Body: Get necessary documents to travel to the U.S.

  V. Body: Research universities and decide which is the best one

VI. Conclusion

ACTIVITY 9 | Writing essay outlines

Work with a small group. Brainstorm ideas for essays with the following thesis statements. Then on a separate piece of paper, write an essay outline for each. Remember to ask a question about the thesis to develop ideas for the body paragraphs. Share your outlines with your class.

  1. Thesis Statement: Computer literacy is important for children for many reasons.

  2. Thesis Statement: To prepare for a vocabulary test, students should take these steps.

Girls secondary school in Oman

ACTIVITY 10 | Completing an outline

Look back at "The Benefits of Being Bilingual" in Activity 8 and complete the outline.

I. Introduction (paragraph 1)

    A. Beginning of Essay

    B. Thesis Statement: _____

    _____

II. Body (paragraph 2) Topic Sentence: _____

    _____

    A. Supporting Idea: *They can travel to more countries with less worry.*

    B. Supporting Idea: *They do not need a translator and can communicate better.*

III. Body (paragraph 3) Topic Sentence: *Speaking a second language also allows people to learn about another culture through the special words and phrases in that language.*

    A. Supporting Idea: *The expression "meat and potatoes" teaches us about what kinds of food this culture values.*

    B. Supporting Idea: *The expressions "to rat on someone" and "to be a rat" teach us that rats do not have a positive image in this culture.*

    C. Supporting Idea: _____

    _____

IV. Body (Paragraph 4) Topic Sentence: _____

    _____

    A. Supporting Idea: *It is easier to understand other people's ideas, beliefs, and actions.*

    B. Supporting Idea: _____

    _____

V. Concluding paragraph (paragraph 5)

    A. Restatement of Thesis: *The benefits of bilingualism are clear.*

    B. Opinion/Prediction: _____

    _____

ACTIVITY 11 | Putting an essay together: Brainstorming

In this activity, you will brainstorm ideas for an essay that you will write in Activity 12.
Read the essay topic. Then follow the steps below to brainstorm ideas for an essay.

Topic: Living in a big city is better than living in a small town.

1. Form three groups. Each group must brainstorm and come up with as many reasons as possible why living in a large city is better than living in a small town.

   Your group's reasons: _____

   _____

   _____

   _____

   _____

   _____

2. Write all your ideas on the board. As a class, vote for the three best reasons. (These reasons will be the information for the topic sentences for the essay you will write in Activity 12.) Each group will brainstorm examples for one reason. Decide which reason each group will write about. Write them below.

   Group 1 reason: _____

   Group 2 reason: _____

   Group 3 reason: _____

3. Brainstorm some examples that support your group's reason (topic sentence).

   _____

   _____

   _____

   _____

4. Share your group's examples with the rest of the class. Fill in the list below.

   Group 1 reason: _____

   Examples: _____

   Group 2 reason: _____

   Examples: _____

   Group 3 reason: _____

   Examples: _____

You are now ready to complete an essay. Complete the partial essay with the information you gathered. Use additional paper if necessary.

> **WORDS TO KNOW** Essay 10.3
>
> **diverse:** (adj) very different
> **mayor:** (n) the leader of a city
> **outweigh:** (v) to be more important than
>
> **routine:** (n) things a person does regularly
> **rural:** (adj) describing the countryside (not a city)

ESSAY 10.3

The Advantages of City Life

1   The population of Small Hills is 2,500. Everyone knows everyone else. The **mayor** of the city is also the owner of the only restaurant. On weekends, many residents go to this restaurant, and perhaps after dinner, they go to the only movie theater. This **routine** continues. On the other hand, the population of Los Angeles is approximately 4 million. It is a culturally **diverse** city where you can eat at any type of restaurant, watch any type of movie, and visit a great number of museums. Clearly, living in a large city is better than living in a small, **rural** community.

2   First, living in a large city is better because _____

_____

_____

_____

3   In addition, city life can _____

_____

_____

_____

4   Finally, large cities give people the opportunity to _____

_____

_____

_____

5   In conclusion, there are many benefits to living in a large city. These benefits are very important to many people. Although some people prefer the slower life in rural areas, the benefits that a large city can offer to its citizens **outweigh** the benefits that a rural area can offer.

Using a Hook to Improve Your Essay

The first thing that good writers want to do is get their readers' attention with an interesting sentence or piece of information. This is called a **hook** because it hooks, or catches, the readers' attention. There are several kinds of hooks, and all of them are good tools.

TYPE OF HOOK	EXAMPLES
A question	Have you ever wondered how a jet with 300 passengers can lift itself from the ground?
A famous quote	John F. Kennedy famously said, "Ask not what your country can do for you. Ask what you can do for your country."
History	Leonardo da Vinci was born and lived his early years in the small town of Vinci. He would sit on a small hill in his village and think about destiny. At the age of 15, his life was changed forever when he became an apprentice for the most famous artist in Florence, Italy.
A surprising statistic	Although there are more than one million wild alligators in the state of Florida, there are only on average seven accidental attacks on humans each year.

ACTIVITY 13 | Putting an essay together: Adding a hook

Look at the introduction paragraph of Essay 10.3, "The Advantages of City Life." On a separate piece of paper, think of and write two or three different hooks to make the essay more interesting. Share your ideas with your class.

ACTIVITY 14 | Peer editing

Work with a partner. Read your partner's essay from Activity 12. Then use Peer Editing Sheet 10 in the *Writer's Handbook*. Offer positive suggestions to help your partner write a better essay. Consider your partner's comments as you revise your essay.

BUILDING BETTER VOCABULARY

WORDS TO KNOW

accomplish (v)	diverse (adj) AW	mayor (n)
basic (adj)	expression (n)	outweigh (v)
bilingual (adj) AW	focus (v) AW	prevent (v)
deadly (adj)	frequently (adv)	routine (n)
decade (n) AW	invention (n)	rural (adj)
discovery (n)	maintain (v) AW	technology (n) AW

ACTIVITY 15 | Word associations

Circle the word or phrase that is more closely related to the bold word on the left.

1. accomplish	do	plan
2. bilingual	two languages	two teams
3. decade	10 years	100 years
4. discovery	found	produced
5. diverse	different	similar
6. expression	listen	say
7. maintain	change	keep
8. mayor	person	thing
9. prevent	begin	stop
10. rural	buildings	nature

ACTIVITY 16 | Collocations

Fill in the blank with the word that most naturally completes the phrase.

bilingual	decade	focus	maintain	prevent

1. _____ a good safety record

2. _____ on a specific issue

3. a _____ dictionary

4. a _____ of economic success

5. to _____ an accident

accomplish	basic	discover	invention	mayor

6. _____ a better way to do something

7. _____ a goal

8. a _____ reason (for something)

9. the _____ of a city

10. a great _____ from the 1920s

ACTIVITY 17 | Word forms

Complete each sentence with the correct word form. Use the correct forms of the words.

NOUN	VERB	ADJECTIVE	SENTENCES
accomplishment	accomplish	accomplished	1. What do you consider to be your greatest _____? 2. It is difficult to _____ much outside the house when you are a full-time parent.
benefit	benefit	beneficial	3. This new plan is _____ to everyone. 4. Can you list at least three _____ of this new plan?
invention inventor	invent	inventive	5. Thomas Edison was a famous _____. 6. Which _____ from the 1800s do you think was the most important?
maintenance	maintain	maintained	7. They _____ the house for us when we are on vacation. 8. The car needs its yearly _____.
prevention	prevent	preventive	9. Some people believe that vitamin C can _____ a cold. 10. The _____ of diseases like malaria is one of our top goals.

ACTIVITY 18 | Vocabulary in writing

Choose five words from Words to Know. Write a complete sentence with each word.

1. _____

_____

2. _____

_____

3. _____

_____

4. _____

_____

5. _____

_____

BUILDING BETTER SENTENCES

ACTIVITY 19 | Editing

Identify and correct the seven errors in this paragraph. The errors are: missing commas (2), missing subject (1), verb tense (2), missing article (1), and word form (1).

Some words do not translate exactly from one language to another. In French, for example, there are two ways to say *know*. One is for knowing a fact and the other is for knowing person. English has the words *make* and *do* but Spanish has only *hacer*. In Spanish, you used *hacer* with a reservation and homework, but this certainly seems strangely to an English speaker. Finally, the English verb *miss* was hard to translate well into some foreign languages. In summary, is hard to translate certain words from one language to another.

ACTIVITY 20 | Scrambled sentences

Unscramble the words and phrases to write complete sentences.

1. accomplish a great / mayor can / her plans / deal if his or / a good / are creative

_____

2. help improve / brought many economic / technology has / benefits that can / modern / people's lives

_____

3. many students prefer / a bilingual / are trying / to learn new / to use / vocabulary / dictionary when they

_____

4. the world / is the computer / one invention / that has / clearly changed

_____

5. been very / for a lot / although cars / of the pollution that / they have / we have today, / important to our daily lives / are responsible

_____

ACTIVITY 21 | Combining sentences

Combine the ideas into one sentence. You may change the word forms, but do not change or omit any ideas. There may be more than one correct answer.

1. Bad weather can cause accidents.
The accidents involve traffic.
Bad weather can cause delays.
The delays involve flights.

_____

_____

2. Buenos Aires is the capital of Argentina.
Buenos Aires is the largest city in Argentina.

_____

_____

3. Oxygen is a gas.
Oxygen is colorless.
Oxygen is odorless.
Oxygen is essential to human life.

_____

_____

WRITING

ACTIVITY 22 | Writing an essay

Write an opinion or process essay. Follow these guidelines.

1. Choose which essay you want to write.

   Opinion Essay: Should high schools require an art class in their curriculum, or should they focus on teaching only academic subjects?

   Process Essay: What are some ways to make new friends?

2. Use at least two of the vocabulary words or phrases from Words to Know.

3. Follow the steps of the writing process in the *Writer's Handbook*.

Additional Topics for Writing

Here are more ideas for essays. When you write your essay, follow the guidelines in Activity 22.

TOPIC 1: Look at the photo at the beginning of the unit. What are the necessary qualities that these dancers must have to be successful?

TOPIC 2: Think about your city or town. Write about how the place has changed in the last 50 years. What specific things are different now?

TOPIC 3: Think about the "best" age for marriage. In your essay, explain the reasons for this perfect age.

TOPIC 4: Write about the best strategies to use when preparing for a big exam. Explain your choices.

TOPIC 5: Write about the value of competition. What does it provide? How is it beneficial? Are there any disadvantages?

TEST PREP

> **TIP**
> Take a few minutes to check your concluding paragraph before you submit your essay. Make sure your it restates information in the introduction paragraph or offers a suggestion, gives an opinion, or makes a prediction. Do not include any new information. This paragraph will help readers better understand and remember your ideas.

You should spend about 50 minutes on this task. Write a short essay about the following topic:

What should happen to students who are caught cheating on an exam? Why?

Start by writing an outline for your essay. Then write a short introduction (with a hook and a thesis statement), two or three well-developed body paragraphs, and a strong conclusion. Include any relevant examples from your own knowledge.

WRITER'S HANDBOOK

LANGUAGE TERMS

Adjective   An adjective describes a noun.

Lexi is a very **smart** girl.

Adverb   An adverb describes a verb, an adjective, or another adverb.

The secretary types **quickly**. She types **very quickly**.

Article   Articles are used with nouns. The definite article is *the*. The indefinite articles are *a* and *an*.

The teacher gave **an** assignment to **the** students.

Clause   A clause is a group of words that has a subject-verb combination. Sentences can have one or more clauses.

      S   V
Roger attends the College of New Jersey.
          clause

   S   V   S   V
Chris needs to study because **he wants** to pass the class.
     clause 1   clause 2

Complex Sentence   A complex sentence consists of an independent clause and a dependent clause. Dependent clauses include time clauses, *if* clauses, and reason clauses.

We will go to lunch as soon as class is over.
   ind clause   dep clause

If you miss the test, you cannot take it again.
   dep clause   ind clause

Chris studies hard because he wants to do well.
   ind clause   dep clause

Compound Sentence   A compound sentence consists of two simple sentences that are joined by a comma and a connector such as *and*, *but*, or *so*.

I love to study English**, but** my sister prefers math.
  simple sentence 1   simple sentence 2

Dependent Clause   A dependent clause is a group of words with a subject-verb combination that cannot be a sentence by itself. It starts with a connector such as *before*, *after*, *if*, or *because*.

I am taking a lot of science classes **because I want to go to medical school**.

Independent Clause	An independent clause is a group of words with a subject-verb combination that can be a sentence by itself.
	I am taking a lot of science classes because I want to go to medical school.
Noun	A noun is a person, place, thing, or idea.
	The **students** are reading **poems** about **friendship** and **love**.
Object	An object is a word that comes after a transitive verb or a preposition. It is often a noun, noun phrase, pronoun, or gerund.
	Jim bought **a new car**.
	I left my jacket in **the house**.
Phrase	A phrase is a small group of words that create a larger unit, such as a noun phrase or prepositional phrase.
	Kimchi is **a traditional Korean dish**.
	Jane forgot her phone **on the bus**.
Preposition	A preposition is a word that shows location, time, or direction. Prepositions are often one word (*at, on, in*), but they can also consist of two words (*in between*) or three words (*on top of*).
	The university is **in** the center of the city.
Pronoun	A pronoun can replace a noun in a sentence. Using a combination of nouns and pronouns adds variety to your writing.
	n subj pronoun
	Whales are mammals. **They** breathe air.
	n obj pronoun
	Some **whales** are endangered. We need to protect **them**.
Punctuation	Punctuation refers to the marks used in writing to separate sentences and parts of sentences and to clarify meaning.
	The colors of the American flag are red, white, and blue, and the colors of the Mexican flag are red, white, and green.
Subject	The subject of a sentence tells who or what a sentence is about. It is often a noun, noun phrase, pronoun, or gerund.
	My teacher gave us a homework assignment. **It** was difficult.

UNDERSTANDING THE WRITING PROCESS

As you know, writing is a process. Most strong writers follow steps such as these when writing. Use these as your guide when you write a paragraph or an essay.

Step 1:   Choose a Topic

Step 2:   Brainstorm

Step 3:   Outline

Step 4:   Write the First Draft

Step 5:   Get Feedback from a Peer

Step 6:   Reread, Rethink, Rewrite

Step 7:   Proofread the Final Draft

This section will show you how a student went through the steps to do complete an assignment. First, read the student's final paragraph and the teacher's comments. Then read the steps the student took to write this final paragraph.

FINAL DRAFT

Gumbo

The Newbury House Dictionary of American English defines gumbo as "a thick soup made with okra and often meat, fish, or vegetables," but anyone who has tasted this delicious dish knows that this definition is too simple to describe gumbo accurately. It is true that gumbo is a thick soup, but it is much more than that. Gumbo, which is one of the most popular of all Louisiana dishes, can be made with many different kinds of ingredients. For example, seafood gumbo usually contains shrimp and crab. Other kinds of gumbo can include chicken, sausage, or turkey. Three other important ingredients that all gumbo recipes use are okra, onions, and green peppers. Regardless of the ingredients in gumbo, this dish from the southern part of Louisiana is one of the most delicious regional foods in the United States.

Teacher comments:
100/A Excellent paragraph! I enjoyed reading about gumbo. Your paragraph is well written. All the sentences relate to one topic. I like that you used so many connectors (e.g., however, such as).

Steps in the Writing Process

Step 1: Choose a Topic

The first step is to read and understand the assignment and choose an appropriate topic to write about. The assignment is: *Write a definition paragraph about a favorite food.* The student chose to write about a food that she loves and that reminds her of home. She chose a dish called *gumbo*, which is a popular dish in her state of Louisiana, USA.

Step 2: Brainstorm

Write every idea about your topic that comes to mind. Some of these ideas will be better than others; write them all. The main purpose of brainstorming is to write as many ideas as possible. If one idea looks promising, circle it or put a check next to it. If you write an idea that you know right away you are not going to use, cross it out.

Brainstorming methods include making lists, making charts, or diagramming ideas (as in the cluster diagram below). This diagram shows a student's brainstorm notes about the topic "gumbo."

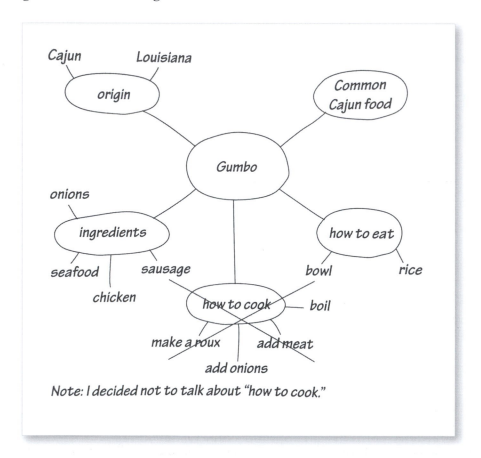

As you can see, the student considered many aspects of the topic, but decided not to write about how to cook gumbo. Each circle on the outside might be supporting ideas and sentences.

Step 3: Outline

The next step is to make an outline. You may want to start writing after brainstorming, but creating an outline first will help you to organize your ideas.

After brainstorming, look at your notes and create a simple outline, or plan, for your writing. Here is an example of a rough outline for the paragraph *Gumbo*.

I.   Topic sentence: What is gumbo?

II. Support (fact, example, or story): Define gumbo: what exactly is it? (a thick soup with various meat/seafood and vegetables)

III. Support (fact, example, or story): Discuss origin of gumbo: where is it from?

IV. Support (fact, example, or story): Discuss different types of gumbo and the ingredients.

V.   Conclusion: Summarize why gumbo is good/special

Step 4: Write the First Draft

In this step, you use information from your brainstorming notes and outline to draft the essay.

When you write your first draft, pay attention to the language you use. Use a variety of sentence types. Consider your choice of vocabulary. Include specific terminology when possible, and avoid using informal or conversational language.

The first draft may contain errors, such as misspellings, incomplete ideas, and punctuation errors. At this point, you should not worry about correcting the errors. The focus should be on putting your ideas into sentences.

As you write the first draft, you may want to add information or take some out. In some cases, your first draft may not follow your outline exactly. That is OK. Writers do not always stick with their original plan or follow the steps in the writing process in order. Sometimes they go back and forth between steps.

FIRST DRAFT

Gumbo

Do you know what gumbo is? It's a seafood soup. However, gumbo is really more than a kind of soup, it's special. Gumbo is one of the most popular of all Cajun dish. It's made with various kinds of seafood or meat. This is mixed with vegetables such as onions, green peppers. Seafood Gumbo is made with shrimp and crab. Also chicken, sausage, and turkey etc. Regardless of what is in Gumbo, it's usually served in bowl over the rice.

Step 5: Get Feedback from a Peer

Peer editing is important in the writing process. You do not always see your own mistakes or places where information is missing because you are too close to the paragraph or essay that you wrote. Ask someone to read your draft and give you feedback about your writing. Choose someone that you trust and feel comfortable with. Your teacher may also give you feedback on your first draft. As you revise, consider all comments carefully.

The following is an example of a completed peer editing form.

Sample Peer Editing Form

Reader: _Jim_   Date: _2/14_

1. What is the topic of the paragraph? _gumbo (a food dish from Louisiana)_

2. Does the paragraph have a topic sentence?   ☐ Yes   ☑ No

   Write it and/or suggest another one: _Do you know what gumbo is? (Maybe make this more._
   interesting Tell us why should read about gumbo.)

3. Do all sentences in the paragraph relate to the topic sentence?   ☑ Yes   ☐ No

   If no, which sentence(s) does not belong? _____

   _____

4. Does the paragraph have a concluding sentence?   ☐ Yes   ☑ No

   Write it and/or suggest a better one _The concluding sentence doesn't restate the topic_
   sentence, state an opinion, or make a suggestion. Maybe suggest that people try gumbo.

5. Do all verbs agree with their subjects?   ☑ Yes   ☐ No

   If no, write errors here or mark them on the paragraph. _____

   _____

6. What do you like best about this paragraph? _I like learning about new foods, especially with_
   ingredients I am not familiar with (e.g., okra).

7. What could the writer do to improve the paragraph? _I'd like to know what flavors or spices_
   are in gumbo. It would be good to know why it is special or why it is delicious.

Step 6: Reread, Rethink, Rewrite

This step consists of three parts:

1. Reread your essay and any comments from your peers or teacher.
2. Rethink your writing and address the comments.
3. Rewrite the essay.

A general checklist to use as you rewrite your work might look like this:

- ☐ Is there a clear topic sentence?
- ☐ Do all sentences relate to the topic sentence?
- ☐ Do the sentences flow?
- ☐ Is there a concluding sentence?
- ☐ Is there a title?

Step 7: Proofread the Final Draft

Proofreading is the final step. It means reading to check for any grammar, punctuation, or spelling errors. One good way to proofread your paper is to set it aside for several hours or a day or two. The next time you read it, your head will be clearer and you will be more likely to see any errors.

A proofreading checklist might look like this:

- ☐ Are your words capitalized correctly?
- ☐ Do you have the correct final punctuation?
- ☐ Are your words spelled correctly?
- ☐ Did you use the correct word forms?

Now go back and read the first draft and final draft of *Gumbo*. Notice the changes from the first draft to the final draft.

CAPITALIZATION AND PUNCTUATION

Capitalization

Capitalize:

- the first word in a sentence

  We go to the movies every week.
  Deserts are beautiful places to visit.

- the pronoun *I*

  Larry and **I** are brothers

- people's formal and professional titles

  Mr. and **M**rs. Jenkins are on vacation.
  Lisa saw **D**r. Johansen at the bank yesterday.

- proper names (specific people, places, and things)

  Kate met her brother **A**lex at the park.
  The **C**oliseum in **R**ome is a beautiful old monument.
  Nick is taking **H**istory 101 this semester.

- names of streets.

  Ruth lives on **W**ilson **A**venue.

- geographical locations (cities, states, countries, continents, lakes, and rivers)

  I am going to travel to **L**ondon, **E**ngland, next week.
  The **A**rno **R**iver passes through **T**uscany, **I**taly.

- the names of languages and nationalities

  My grandmother speaks Polish.
  Melissa is Venezuelan, but her husband is Cuban.

- most words in titles of paragraphs, essays, and books

  *The **L**ife of **B**illy **B**arnes*
  *Into the **W**ild*

End Punctuation

The most common punctuation marks found at the end of English sentences are the **period**, the **question mark**, and the **exclamation point**. It is important to know how to use all three of them correctly. Of these three, the period is by far the most commonly used punctuation mark.

1. **period** (.) A period is used at the end of a declarative sentence.

   This sentence is a declarative sentence.
   This sentence is not a question.

2. **question mark** (?) A question mark is used at the end of a question.

   Is this idea difficult?
   How many questions are in this group?

3. **exclamation point** (!) An exclamation point is used at the end of an exclamation. It expresses a strong emotion. It is less common than the other two marks.

   I cannot believe you think this topic is difficult!
   This is the best writing book in the world!

Commas

Use a comma:

• **before the connectors** *and*, *but*, *so*, **and** *or* **in a compound sentence.**

   Rick bought Julia a croissant, but she wanted a muffin

• **between three or more items in a list.**

   Jen brought a towel, an umbrella, some sunscreen, and a book to the beach.

• **after a dependent clause at the beginning of a complex sentence. Dependent clauses include time clauses,** *if* **clauses, and reason clauses.**

   Because it was raining outside, Alex used his umbrella.

• **between the day and the date and between the date and the year.**

   The last day of class will be Friday, May 19th.
   I was born on June 27, 1992.

• **between and after (if in the middle of a sentence) city, state, and country names that appear together.**

   The concert was in Busan, Korea.
   I lived in Phuket, Thailand, for ten years.

• **after time words and phrases, prepositional phrases of time, and sequence words (except** *then***) at the start of a sentence.**

   Every afternoon after school, I go to the library.
   Finally, they decided to ask the police for help.

Apostrophes

Apostrophes have two basic uses in English. They indicate either a contraction or a possession. Note that contractions are seldom used in academic writing.

1. Contractions: Use an apostrophe in a contraction in place of the letter or letters that have been deleted. <u>Do not use contractions in academic writing</u>.

> He's (he is or he has), they're (they are), I've (I have), we'd (we would or we had)

2. Possession: Add an apostrophe and the letter *s* after the word. If a plural word already ends in *s*, then just add an apostrophe.

> yesterday's paper
> the boy's books (One boy has some books.)
> the boys' books (Several boys have one or more books.)

Quotation Marks

Here are three of the most common uses for quotation marks.

1. **To mark the exact words that were spoken by someone. Notice that the period and comma at the end of a quote are inside the quotation marks.**

   > The king said, "I refuse to give up my throne."
   > "None of the solutions is correct," said the professor.

2. **To mark language that a writer has borrowed from another source.**

   > The dictionary defines gossip as a "talk or writing about other people's actions or lives, sometimes untruthful," but I would add that it is usually mean.

3. **To indicate when a word or phrase is being used in a special way.**

   > The king believed himself to be the leader of a democracy, so he allowed the prisoner to choose his method of dying. According to the king, allowing this kind of "democracy" showed that he was indeed a good ruler.

ARTICLES

The Indefinite Articles *A* and *An*

Use *a* or *an* before a singular count noun when its meaning is general. Use *a* before a word that starts with a consonant sound. Use *an* before a word that starts with a vowel sound.

Words that begin with the letters *h* and *u* can take *a* or *an* depending on their opening sound.
- **When the *h* is pronounced, use *a*.**

  a horse / **a** hat / **a** hot day / **a** huge dog

- **When the *h* is silent, use *an*.**

  an hour / **an** honor / **an** honourable man / **an** herb

- **When the *u* sounds like the word *you*, use *a*.**

  a university / **a** uniform / **a** useful invention / **a** unique idea

- **When the *u* sounds like *uh*, use *an*.**

  an umpire / **an** umbrella / **an** ugly shirt / **an** uncomfortable chair

Definite Article *The*

Use *the*:
- before a singular count noun, plural count noun, or non-count noun when its meaning is specific.

  I need to ask my parents to borrow **the car** today.

- the second (and third, fourth, etc.) time you write about something.

  I bought a new coat yesterday. **The coat** is blue and gray.

- when the noun you are referring to is unique—there is only one.

  The Sun and **the Earth** are both in **the Milky Way Galaxy**.
  The Eiffel Tower is beautiful.

- with specific time periods.

  You must be very quiet for **the next hour**.
  The 1920s was a time of great change in the United States.

- when other words in your sentence make the noun specific.

  The cat in **the picture** is very pretty.

- with geographic locations that end in the plural -*s* (such as a group of islands), or the words *united, union, kingdom,* or *republic.*

> We are going to **the Bahamas** for our vacation.
> Who is the president of **the United States**?

- with most buildings, bodies of water (except lakes), mountain chains, and deserts.

> **The White House** is in Washington, DC.
> **The Amazon** is a very long river in South America.

Do not use *the*:

- with the names of cities, states, countries, continents, and lakes (except as mentioned above).

> Sylvie is from **Venezuela**. She lives near **Lake Maracaibo**.
> **Lake Baikal** is a large freshwater lake in **Russia**.

- before names or when you talk about something in general

> **Leo Tolstoy** is a famous Russian writer.
> **Jason** is going to make a table with **wood**.

SENTENCE TYPES

English has three types of sentences: simple, compound, and complex. These labels indicate how the information in a sentence is organized, not how difficult the content is.

Simple Sentences

Simple sentences usually contain one subject and one verb.

>   S   V
> <u>Children</u> <u>love</u> electronic devices.

>   V   S   V
> <u>Does</u> <u>this</u> <u>sound</u> like a normal routine?

Sometimes simple sentences can contain more than one subject or verb.

>   S   S   V
> <u>Brazil</u> and <u>the United States</u> <u>are</u> large countries.

>   S   V   V
> <u>Brazil</u> <u>is</u> in South America and <u>has</u> a large population.

Compound Sentences

Compound sentences are usually made up of two simple sentences (independent clauses). The two sentences are connected with a coordinating conjunction such as *and, but, or, yet, so,* and *for.*

A comma is often used before the coordinating conjunction.

Megan studied hard, **but** she did not pass the final test.

More and more people are shopping online, **so** many stores have been forced to close.

The administration will use the funds to purchase new computers, **or** it will use them to remodel the school cafeteria.

Complex Sentences

Complex sentences contain one independent clause and at least one dependent clause. In most complex sentences, the dependent clause is an adverb clause. (Other complex sentences have dependent adjective clauses or dependent noun clauses.)

Adverb clauses begin with subordinating conjunctions, such as *while, although, because,* and *if.*

Study the examples below. The adverb clauses are underlined, and the subordinating conjunctions are boldfaced. Notice that the subordinating conjunctions are part of the dependent clauses.

independent clause   dependent clause

The hurricane struck **while** we were at the mall.

dependent clause   independent clause

After the president gave his speech, he answered the reporters' questions.

Dependent clauses must be attached to an independent clause. They cannot stand alone as a sentence. If they are not attached to another sentence, they are called fragments, or incomplete sentences. Look at these examples:

Fragment: After the president gave his speech.

Complete Sentence: After the president gave his speech, he answered the questions.

Fragment: Although every citizen is entitled to vote.

Complete Sentence: Although every citizen is entitled to vote, many do not.

CONNECTORS

Using connectors will help your ideas flow. Three types of connectors are coordinating conjunctions, subordinating conjunctions, and transitions.

Coordinating Conjunctions

Coordinating conjunctions join two independent clauses to form a compound sentence. Use a comma before a coordinating conjunction in a compound sentence.

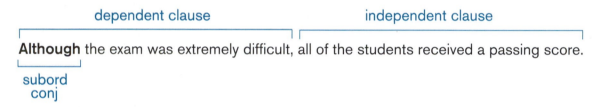

| Independent clause | coord conj | independent clause |

The exam was extremely difficult, **but** all of the students received a passing score.

Subordinating Conjunctions

Subordinating conjunctions introduce a dependent clause in a complex sentence. When a dependent clause begins a sentence, use a comma to separate it from the independent clause.

| dependent clause | independent clause |

Although the exam was extremely difficult, all of the students received a passing score.

subord conj

When a dependent clause comes after an independent clause, no comma is used.

| independent clause | dependent clause |

All of the students received a passing score **although** the exam was extremely difficult.

subord conj

Transition Words

Transition words show the relationship between ideas in sentences. A transition followed by a comma often begins a sentence.

| independent clause | transition | independent clause |

The exam was extremely difficult. **However**, all of the students received a passing score.

Connector Summary Chart

PURPOSE	COORDINATING CONJUNCTIONS	SUBORDINATING CONJUNCTIONS	TRANSITION WORDS
To give an example			For example, To illustrate, Specifically, In particular
To add information	and		In addition, Moreover, Furthermore
To signal a comparison			Similarly, Likewise, In the same way
To signal a contrast	but yet	while, although	In contrast, However, On the other hand, Instead
To signal a concession	yet	although, though, even though	Nevertheless, Even so, Admittedly, Despite this
To emphasize			In fact, Actually
To clarify			In other words, In simpler words, More simply
To give a reason/cause	for	because, since	
To show a result	so	so	As a result, Therefore, Thus
To show time relationships		after, as soon as, before, when, while, until, since, whenever, as	Afterward, First, Second, Next, Then, Finally, Subsequently, Meanwhile, In the meantime
To signal a condition		if, even if, unless, provided that, when	
To signal a purpose		so that, in order that	
To signal a choice	or		
To signal a conclusion			In conclusion, To summarize, As we have seen, In brief, In closing, To sum up, Finally

USEFUL WORDS AND PHRASES

COMPARING	
Comparative Adjective	New York is **larger** than Rhode Island.
Comparative Adverb	A jet flies **faster** than a helicopter.
In comparison,	Canada has provinces. **In comparison,** Brazil has states.
Compared to Similar to Like	**Compared to** these roses, those roses last a long time.
Both … and	**Both** models **and** real planes have similar controls.
Likewise, Similarily,	Good writers spend hours each day developing their language skills to enhance their writing. **Likewise,** good ballerinas spend countless hours in the gym each week increasing their accuracy and endurance.

CONTRASTING	
In contrast, …	Algeria is a very large country. **In contrast,** the U.A.E. is very small.
Contrasted with In contrast to	**In contrast to** Chicago, Miami has only two seasons: a very mild winter and a very long summer.
Although Even though Though	**Though** London in 1900 was quite different from London in 2000 in many ways, important similarities existed in population, technology, and transportation.
Unlike	**Unlike** Chicago, the problem in Miami is not the cold but rather the heat.
However,	Canada has provinces. **However,** Brazil has states.
On the one hand, On the other hand,	**On the one hand,** Maggie loved to travel. **On the other hand,** she hated to be away from her home.

SHOWING CAUSE AND EFFECT

Because Since	**Because** their races are longer, distance runners need to be mentally strong.
cause lead to result in	An earthquake can **cause** tidal waves which often **lead to** massive destruction.
As a result of Because of	**Because of** the economic sanctions, the unemployment rate rose.
Therefore, As a result,	Markets fell. **Therefore,** millions of people lost their life savings.

STATING AN OPINION

I believe / think / feel / agree / that	**I believe that** using electronic devices on a plane should be allowed.
In my opinion / view / experience,	**In my opinion,** talking on a cell phone in a movie theater is extremely rude.
For this reason,	**For this reason,** voters should not pass this law.
There are many benefits / advantages / disadvantages	**There are many benefits** to swimming every day.

ARGUING

It is important to remember that	**It is important to remember that** school uniforms would only be worn during school hours.
According to a recent survey,	**According to a recent survey,** the biggest fear of most people is public speaking.
For these reasons,	**For these reasons,** public schools should require uniforms.
Without a doubt,	**Without a doubt,** students ought to learn a foreign language.

VERB FORMS AND USES

VERB FORM	USE	EXAMPLES
Simple Present	▪ regular activities or habits ▪ facts or things that are generally true	He **teaches** three classes on Wednesdays. The moon **goes** around the Earth every 27.3 days.
Simple Past	▪ recent or historical events ▪ a narrative, or story, that is real or imagined ▪ events in a person's life ▪ the result of an experiment	The semester **ended** a week ago. Cinderella **lost** her shoe. George Washington **grew up** in Virginia. Some children **ate** the marshmallow and others **did not eat** it until later. The children **were** more successful in life if they **waited** to eat the marshmallow.
Present Progressive	▪ actions that are currently in progress ▪ future actions if a future time expression is used or understood	The sun **is shining**. We **are meeting** Friday in the library.
Future with *be going to*	▪ future plans that are already made ▪ predictions	They **are going to visit** Thailand and Malaysia on their trip. The storm **is going to be** dangerous.
Future with *will*	▪ future plans/decisions made in the moment ▪ strong predictions ▪ promises and offers to help	I **will bring** some snacks. The storm **will destroy** homes. She **will support** the rights of all people.
Present Perfect	▪ actions that began in the past and continue until the present ▪ an action that happened at an indefinite time in the past ▪ repeated actions at indefinite times in the past	She **has studied** here for two years. They **have visited** the museum already. There **have been** several hurricanes this year.

TEST TAKING TIPS

Before Writing

- Before you begin writing, make sure that you understand the assignment. Underline key words in the writing prompt. Look back at the key words as you write to be sure you are answering the question correctly and staying on topic.
- Take five minutes to plan before you start writing. First, list out all the ideas you have about the topic. Then think about which ideas have the best supporting examples or ideas. Use this information to choose your main idea(s). Circle the supporting information you want to include. Cross out other information.
- Organize your ideas before you write. Review the list you have created. Place a number next to each idea, from most important to least important. In this way, if you do not have enough time to complete your writing, you will be sure that the most relevant information will be included in your essay.

While Writing

For Paragraphs

- Be sure that your topic sentence has a logical controlling idea. Remember that your topic sentence guides your paragraph. If the topic sentence is not clear, the reader will have difficulty following your supporting ideas.
- It is important for your writing to look like a paragraph. Be sure to indent the first sentence. Write the rest of the sentences from margin to margin. Leave an appropriate amount of space after your periods. These small details make your paragraph easier to read and understand.

For Essays

- Be sure that your thesis statement responds to the prompt and expresses your main idea. The thesis may also include your points of development. Remember that if your thesis statement is not clear, the reader will have difficulty following the supporting ideas in the body paragraphs.
- Readers will pay special attention to the last paragraph of your essay, so take two or three minutes to check it before you submit it. Make sure your concluding paragraph restates information in the introduction paragraph and offers a suggestion, gives an opinion, asks a question, or makes a prediction.

For Either Paragraphs or Essays

- Do not write more than is requested. If the assignment asks for a 150-word response, be sure that your writing response comes close to that. Students do not get extra points for writing more than what is required.
- If you are using a word processor, choose a font that is academic and clear like Times New Roman or Calibri. Choose an appropriate point size like 12. Use double space or one and a half space so that it is easier to read. Remember to indent paragraphs and leave a space between sentences.

- Once you pick a side (agree or disagree), include only the ideas that support that side. Sometimes you may have ideas for both sides. If this happens, choose the side that is easier for you to write about. If you do not have an opinion, choose the side you can write about best, even if you do not believe in it. You receive points for your writing skill, not your true personal beliefs.

Word Choice

- Avoid using words such as *always*, *never*, *all*, and *none*. You cannot give enough proof for these words. Instead, use words such as *probably*, *often*, *most*, *many*, *almost never*, and *almost none*.
- Avoid using general or vague vocabulary. Words such as *nice*, *good*, and *very* can often be changed to more specific terms, such as *friendly*, *fabulous*, and *incredibly*. Be more specific in your word choice.
- Avoid conversational or informal language in academic writing.

Development

- Avoid information that is too general. When possible, give specific examples. Good writers want to show that they have thought about the subject and provide interesting and specific information in their writing.

After Writing

- Leave time to proofread your paragraph or essay. Check for subject-verb agreement, correct use of commas and end punctuation, and for clear ideas that all relate to the topic sentence (paragraphs) or thesis statement (essay).
- Check for informal language such as contractions or slang. These do not belong in academic writing.

Managing Time

- It is common to run out of time at the end of a writing test. Once you have written your introduction and the body paragraphs, check your remaining time. Then read through what you have written to check for the clarity of your ideas. If you are running out of time, write a very brief conclusion.

PEER EDITING FORMS

Peer Editing Form 1

Reader: _____ Date: _____

1. What is the topic of the paragraph? _____

2. Does the paragraph have a topic sentence? ☐ Yes ☐ No

   Write it or suggest a better one. _____

   _____

3. Do all sentences in the paragraph relate to the topic sentence? ☐ Yes ☐ No

   If no, write any sentence that does not belong (or mark all on the paragraph).

   _____

   _____

4. Do all verbs agree with their subjects? ☐ Yes ☐ No

   If no, mark any that are incorrect in the paragraph.

5. Does the paragraph have a concluding sentence? ☐ Yes ☐ No

   Write it or suggest a better one. _____

   _____

6. What do you like best about this paragraph? _____

   _____

7. What could the writer do to improve the paragraph? _____

   _____

Peer Editing Form 2

Reader: _____   Date: _____

1. What is the topic of the paragraph? _____

2. Does the paragraph have a topic sentence?   ☐ Yes   ☐ No

   Write it or suggest a better one. _____

   _____

3. Do all sentences in the paragraph relate to the topic sentence?   ☐ Yes   ☐ No

   If no, write any sentence that does not belong (or mark all on the paragraph).

   _____

   _____

4. Do all verbs agree with their subjects?   ☐ Yes   ☐ No

   If no, mark any that are incorrect in the paragraph.

5. Does the paragraph have a concluding sentence?   ☐ Yes   ☐ No

   Write it or suggest a better one. _____

   _____

6. Are there any descriptive adjectives?   ☐ Yes   ☐ No

   If no, show in the paragraph places where some could possibly be added.

7. Does the paragraph have a strong title?   ☐ Yes   ☐ No

   Write it or suggest a better one. _____

8. What do you like best about this paragraph? _____

   _____

9. What could the writer do to improve the paragraph? _____

   _____

Peer Editing Form 3

Reader: _____ Date: _____

1. What is the topic of the paragraph? _____

2. Does the paragraph have a topic sentence with a clear controlling idea? ☐ Yes ☐ No

   If no, suggest a better one. _____

   _____

3. Do all sentences in the paragraph relate to the topic sentence? ☐ Yes ☐ No

   If no, write any sentence that does not belong (or mark all on the paragraph).

   _____

   _____

4. Do all verbs agree with their subjects? ☐ Yes ☐ No

   If no, mark any that are incorrect in the paragraph.

5. Does the paragraph have a concluding sentence? ☐ Yes ☐ No

   Write it or suggest a better one. _____

   _____

6. Does the paragraph have a strong title? ☐ Yes ☐ No

   Write it or suggest a better one. _____

7. What do you like best about this paragraph? _____

   _____

8. What could the writer do to improve the paragraph? _____

   _____

Peer Editing Form 4

Reader: _____ Date: _____

1. What is the topic of the paragraph? _____

2. Does the paragraph have a topic sentence with a clear controlling idea?   ☐ Yes   ☐ No

   If no, suggest a better one: _____

   _____

3. Do all sentences in the paragraph relate to the topic sentence?   ☐ Yes   ☐ No

   If no, write any sentence that does not belong (or mark all on the paragraph).

   _____

   _____

4. Do all verbs agree with their subjects?   ☐ Yes   ☐ No

   If no, mark any that are incorrect in the paragraph.

5. Does the paragraph have a concluding sentence that restates the topic, offers a suggestion,

   gives an opinion, or makes a prediction about it?   ☐ Yes   ☐ No

   Write it or suggest a better one. _____

   _____

6. Does the paragraph have a strong title?   ☐ Yes   ☐ No

   Write it or suggest a better one. _____

7. Do all pronouns refer to nouns correctly?   ☐ Yes   ☐ No

   If no, circle ones that you question.

8. Are there any fragments, run-ons, or comma splices?   ☐ Yes   ☐ No

   If yes, underline and mark them with FR, RO, or CS to indicate the error.

9. What do you like best about this paragraph? _____

   _____

10. What could the writer do to improve the paragraph? _____

   _____

Peer Editing Form 5

Reader: _____ Date: _____

1. What is the topic of the paragraph? _____

2. Does the paragraph have a topic sentence with a clear controlling idea?   ☐ Yes   ☐ No

   If no, suggest a better one: _____
   _____

3. Do all sentences in the paragraph relate to the topic sentence?   ☐ Yes   ☐ No

   If no, write any sentence that does not belong (or mark all on the paragraph).
   _____
   _____

4. Do all verbs agree with their subjects?   ☐ Yes   ☐ No

   If no, mark any that are incorrect in the paragraph.

5. Does the paragraph have a concluding sentence that restates the topic, offers a suggestion,

   gives an opinion, or makes a prediction about it?   ☐ Yes   ☐ No

   Write it or suggest a better one. _____
   _____

6. Does the paragraph have a strong title?   ☐ Yes   ☐ No

   Write it or suggest a better one. _____

7. Do all pronouns refer to nouns correctly?   ☐ Yes   ☐ No

   If no, circle ones that you question.

8. Are there any fragments, run-ons, or comma splices?   ☐ Yes   ☐ No

   If yes, underline and mark them with FR, RO, or CS to indicate the error.

9. What do you like best about this paragraph? _____
   _____

10. What could the writer do to improve the paragraph? _____
    _____

Peer Editing Form 6

Reader: _____ Date: _____

1. What is the topic of the paragraph? _____

2. Does the paragraph have a topic sentence with a clear controlling idea?   ☐ Yes   ☐ No

    Write it or suggest a better one. _____

    _____

3. Do all sentences in the paragraph relate to the topic sentence?   ☐ Yes   ☐ No

    If no, write any sentence that does not belong (or mark all on the paragraph).

    _____

    _____

4. Do all verbs agree with their subjects?   ☐ Yes   ☐ No

    If no, mark any that are incorrect in the paragraph.

5. Does the paragraph have a concluding sentence that restates the topic or makes a prediction

    about it?   ☐ Yes   ☐ No

    Write it or suggest a better one. _____

    _____

6. Does the paragraph have a strong title?   ☐ Yes   ☐ No

    Write it or suggest a better one. _____

7. Are quotations and other punctuation used correctly?   ☐ Yes   ☐ No

    If no, mark any errors in the paragraph.

8. Are there a variety of sentences in the paragraph?   ☐ Yes   ☐ No

    If no, mark places where sentences could be combined.

9. What do you like best about this paragraph? _____

    _____

10. What could the writer do to improve the paragraph? _____

    _____

Peer Editing Form 7

Reader: _____ Date: _____

1. What is the topic of the paragraph? _____

2. Does the paragraph have a topic sentence with a clear controlling idea? ☐ Yes ☐ No

   Write it or suggest a better one. _____

   _____

3. Do all sentences in the paragraph relate to the topic sentence? ☐ Yes ☐ No

   If no, write any sentence that does not belong (or mark all on the paragraph).

   _____

   _____

4. Do all verbs agree with their subjects? ☐ Yes ☐ No

   If no, mark any that are incorrect in the paragraph.

5. Does the paragraph have a concluding sentence that restates the topic, offers a suggestion,

   gives an opinion, or makes a prediction about it? ☐ Yes ☐ No

   Write it or suggest a better one. _____

   _____

6. Does the paragraph have a strong title? ☐ Yes ☐ No

   Write it or suggest a better one. _____

7. Is the sequence of the process clear? ☐ Yes ☐ No

   If no, suggest words or phrases to make it clearer.

8. Is the imperative used when giving the steps of the process? ☐ Yes ☐ No

   If no, circle any errors or suggest places the imperative might be used.

9. What do you like best about this paragraph? _____

   _____

10. What could the writer do to improve the paragraph? _____

   _____

Peer Editing Form 8

Reader: _____ Date: _____

1. What is the topic of the paragraph? _____

2. Does the paragraph have a topic sentence that states a clear opinion? ☐ Yes ☐ No

   Write it or suggest a better one. _____

   _____

3. Do all sentences in the paragraph relate to the topic sentence? ☐ Yes ☐ No

   If no, write any sentence that does not belong (or mark all on the paragraph).

   _____

   _____

4. Do all verbs agree with their subjects? ☐ Yes ☐ No

   If no, mark any that are incorrect in the paragraph.

5. Does the paragraph have a concluding sentence that restates the topic, offers a suggestion,

   gives an opinion, or makes a prediction about it? ☐ Yes ☐ No

   Write it or suggest a better one. _____

   _____

6. Does the paragraph have a strong title? ☐ Yes ☐ No

   Write it or suggest a better one. _____

7. Does the paragraph include facts or stories to support the opinion? ☐ Yes ☐ No

8. Are the word forms correct? ☐ Yes ☐ No

   If no, mark any that are incorrect in the paragraph.

9. What do you like best about this paragraph? _____

   _____

10. What could the writer do to improve the paragraph? _____

    _____

Peer Editing Form 9

Reader: _____   Date: _____

1. What is the topic of the paragraph? _____

2. Does the paragraph have a topic sentence with a clear controlling idea?   ☐ Yes   ☐ No

   Write it or suggest a better one. _____

   _____

3. Does the paragraph tell a story, with a clear beginning, middle, and end?   ☐ Yes   ☐ No

   If no, what could improve? _____

   _____

   _____

4. Do all verbs agree with their subjects?   ☐ Yes   ☐ No

   If no, mark any that are incorrect in the paragraph.

5. Does the narrative have a strong ending?   ☐ Yes   ☐ No

   If no, suggest an idea for a better one. _____

   _____

6. Does the paragraph have a strong title?   ☐ Yes   ☐ No

   Write it or suggest a better one. _____

7. What do you like best about this paragraph? _____

   _____

8. What could the writer do to improve the paragraph? _____

   _____

Peer Editing Form 10

Reader: _____ Date: _____

1. What is the topic of the essay? _____

2. Does the essay have an introduction paragraph with a clear thesis? ☐ Yes ☐ No

   If no, suggest an idea for improving it. _____

   _____

3. Does the introduction have a strong hook? ☐ Yes ☐ No

   If no, suggest an idea for improving it. _____

   _____

4. Do all paragraphs support the essay? ☐ Yes ☐ No

   If no, which paragraph(s)? _____

5. Do all sentences in each paragraph of the essay relate to its topic sentence? ☐ Yes ☐ No

   If no, cross out unrelated sentences.

6. Does the essay have a concluding paragraph? ☐ Yes ☐ No

7. Does the essay have a strong title? ☐ Yes ☐ No

   Write it or suggest a better one. _____

8. What do you like best about this essay? _____

   _____

9. What could the writer do to improve the essay? _____

   _____

VOCABULARY INDEX

Word	Page	CEFR† Level	Word	Page	CEFR† Level
task*	158	B2	used to	69	B1
technology*	175	B1	valid*	165	B2
therefore	55	B1	valuable	161	B1
thick	105	B1	versus	140	C1
traditional*	10	B1	volunteer*	142	B2
translation*	124	B1	waste time	141	B1
tremendously	69	B2	wonder	165	B1
trillion	148	off-list			
unexpected	161	B1			
unless	69	B1			

Every unit in *Great Writing* highlights key academic vocabulary, indicated by **AW**. These words have been selected using the Academic Word List (Coxhead, 2000) and the New Academic Word List (Browne, C., Culligan, B. & Phillips, J., 2013).

*These words are on the AWL or NAWL.

†Vocabulary was also chosen based on levels of The Common European Framework of Reference for Languages (CEFR). CEFR is an international standard for describing language proficiency. *Great Writing 2* is most appropriate for students at CEFR level B1.

The target vocabulary is at the CEFR levels as shown.

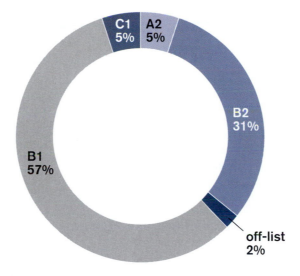

INDEX

CREDITS

Cover © Scott Stringham photographer/Moment/Getty Images

Unit 01 Page 2-3: © Jon Arnold/AWL Images/Getty Images; Page 4: © Giuseppe Ramos/Alamy Stock Photo; Page 5: © Ramon Coloma Mozos/Moment/Getty Images; Page 9: © Danila/Shutterstock.com; Page 11: © Spencer Grant/Science Source/Getty Images; Page 12: © Jesse Kraft/Alamy Stock Photo; Page 13: © tofino/Alamy Stock Photo; Page 15: © Roland Nagy/Alamy Stock Photo; Page 15: © Prasit photo/Moment/Getty Images; Page 16: © Matt Moyer; Page 21: © Srdjan Rakonjac/Alamy Stock Photo

Unit 02 Page 24-25: © Scott Stulberg/Corbis/Getty Images; Page 30: © SinghaphanAllB/Moment/Getty Images; Page 32: © Chamois/iStock/Getty Images; Page 32: © Lisa Tokieda/EyeEm/Getty Images; Page 35: © Monkey Business Images/Shutterstock.com; Page 41: © Todd Bannor/Alamy Stock Photo

Unit 03 Page 44-45: © Jeremy Lasky; Page 46: © Laurentiu Garofeanu/Barcroft Media/Getty Images; Page 51: © NitheshM/iStock/Getty Images; Page 55: © Patricia Dulasi/Shutterstock.com; Page 60: © Johan Swanepoel/Shutterstock.com; Page 52: © Aurora Photos/Alamy Stock Photo

Unit 04 Page: © Patrick Foto/Getty Images; Page 65: © traveler1116/E+/Getty Images; Page 66: © Alexander Mazurkevich/Shutterstock.com; Page 69: © Anna Ivanova/Alamy Stock Photo; Page 70: © Itan1409/Shutterstock.com; Page 71: © Alfa Photostudio/Shutterstock.com; Page 77: © NOAA/Getty Images News/Getty Images; Page 81: © blickwinkel/Alamy Stock Photo

Unit 05 Page 84-85: © AARON HUEY/National Geographic Image Collection; Page 87: © José Fuste Raga/AGE Fotostock; Page 90: © Thomas Linkel/laif/Redux; Page 92: © redswept/Shutterstock.com; Page 95: © Blend Images/Superstock; Page 99: © Keith Ladzinski/National Geographic Image Collection; Page 89: © Design Pics Inc/Alamy Stock Photo; Page 91: © NaturaLight/Alamy Stock Photo

Unit 06 Page: © Jobit George; Page 106: © Alexander Mychko/Alamy Stock Photo; Page 109: © Mike Theiss/National Geographic Image Collection; Page 111: © Joel Sartore/National Geographic Image Collection; Page 113: © membio/Deposit Photos; Page 117: © Piriya Photography/Moment Open/Getty Images

Unit 07 Page 120-121: © Paul Nicklen/National Geographic Image Collection; Page 123: © Steve Debenport/E+/Getty Images; Page 124: © AMNON EICHELBERG/National Geographic Image Collection; Page 126: © gilaxia/E+/Getty Images; Page 126: © gilaxia/iStock/Getty Images; Page 128: © Imgorthand/E+/Getty Images; Page 129: © Reeder Studios, LLC/Alamy Stock Photo

Unit 08 Page 136-137: © Justin Hofman; Page 138: © Dan Rentea/Shutterstock.com; Page 141: © SolStock/Getty Images; Page 142: © Africa Studio/Shutterstock.com; Page 145: © gradyreese/E+/Getty Images; Page 148: © Motortion Films/Shutterstock.com

Unit 09 Page 156-157: © Ilya Varlamov; Page 158: © Steve Debenport/E+/Getty Images; Page 161: © CORY RICHARDS/National Geographic Image Collection; Page 163: © Joel Sartore/National Geographic Image Collection; Page 165: © Roman Samborskyi/Shutterstock.com; Page 166: © Megan Maloy/Image Source/Getty Images

Unit 10 Page 172-173: © John Stanmeyer; Page 177: © Ian Lishman/Juice Images/Alamy Stock Photo; Page 180: © AP Images/Alisha Jucevic; Page 182: © Annie Griffiths